READING JUNG

American Academy of Religion
Studies in Religion

Charley Hardwick and
James O. Duke, Editors

Chuang Tzu: World Philosopher at Play — Kuang-ming Wu

Boundaries in Mind: A Study of Immediate Awareness Based on Psychotherapy — Charles E. Scott

Deconstructing Theology — Mark C. Taylor

The Study of American Indian Religions — Åke Hultkrantz

Evil and the Unconscious — Walter Lowe

God's Activity in the World: The Contemporary Debate — Owen C. Thomas, editor

Reading Freud: Psychology, Neurosis and Religion — Volney P. Gay

Horace Bushnell: Selected Writings on Language, Religion, and American Culture — David L. Smith

Reading Jung: Science, Psychology, and Religion — Volney P. Gay

To Secure the Blessings of Liberty: American Constitutional Law and the New Religious Movements — William C. Shepherd

READING JUNG
Science, Psychology, and Religion

VOLNEY P. GAY

Scholars Press
Chico, California

READING JUNG
Science, Psychology, and Religion

by
Volney P. Gay

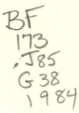

©1984
American Academy of Religion

Library of Congress Cataloging in Publication Data

Gay, Volney Patrick.
  Reading Jung.

  (Studies in religion ; 34)
  Bibliography: p.
  Includes Index.
  1. Jung,   C.   G.   (Carl   Gustav),   1875–1961.
2. Psychoanalysis.   3. Psychoanalysis   and   religion.
I. Title.   II. Series: Studies   in   religion   (American
Academy of Religion) ; no. 34.
BF173.J85G38 1984   150.19′54   84–1322
ISBN 0–89130–731–1

Printed in the United States of America

FOR ELIZABETH

CONTENTS

Acknowledgments ix

Introduction: The Goals of This Book xi

    Jung the Man and Jung the Scientist
    Jung's Goals and Methods
    Texts and References Used
    How to Use This Book

I   Jung's Early Period: Psychiatric Studies 1

    On the Psychology and Pathology of So-Called Occult
        Phenomena (1902) CW 1
    "On Hysterical Misreading" (1904),
        "Cryptomnesia" (1905) CW 1
    "Experimental Researches" (1904–1907) CW 2
    "The Associations of Normal Subjects" (1904) CW 2
    "Psychoanalysis and Association Experiments" (1906) CW 2
    "Association, Dream, and Hysterical Symptom" (1906) CW 2

II   Symbols of Transformation: The Break with Freud 25

    Symbols of Transformation (1911/12) CW 5

III   The Advent of Analytical Psychology: Basic Theorems 45

    "The Theory of Psychoanalysis" (1913) CW 4
    "Psychoanalysis and Neurosis" (1916) CW 4
    "Correspondence between Dr. Jung and Dr. Loy"
        (1914) CW 4
    "Prefaces to 'Collected Papers on Analytical
        Psychology'"(1916) CW 4
    "The Transcendent Function" (1916) CW 8
    "Instinct and the Unconscious" (1919) CW 8
    "The Role of the Unconscious" (1918) CW 10
    "General Aspects of Dream Psychology" (1916) CW 8
    "The Structure of the Unconscious" (1916) CW 7

IV   Psychology of Religion 81

Psychology and Religion (1938) CW 11
"A Psychological Approach to the Trinity" (1942) CW 11
"Transformation Symbolism in the Mass" (1942) CW 11
"On Synchronicity" (1952) CW 8
Aion: Researches Into the Phenomenology of the Self
    (1951) CW 9.2
Answer to Job (1952) CW 11

V   Individuation and Self in *Memories,*
        Dreams, Reflections (1961) 113

Appendix: Research Bibliographies on Jung
and Analytical Psychology 123

Index 143

ACKNOWLEDGEMENTS

I wish to thank the University Research Council of Vanderbilt University for expediting the appearance of this book. I also thank my chairperson, Daniel Patte, and my Dean, Jacque Voegeli, for granting me release time from teaching. In addition, the staff of the Vanderbilt Computer Center, particularly Maria Perkins, made easy what seemed originally difficult. I enjoyed the service of two excellent research assistants, Bruce Vaughn and Kathryn Armistead, and one excellent secretary, Patricia Mundy. The errors and oversights which escaped my detection are, of course, mine alone. I also thank Professor Charley D. Hardwick and an anonymous reviewer who assessed the original manuscript. My greatest debt is to many students from whom I have received more than I have given.

INTRODUCTION

The Goals of This Book

This book is a companion volume to my *Reading Freud: Psychology, Neurosis, Religion* (1983, Scholars Press). Both books have a common goal: to offer the serious student and scholar a systematic way of reading critically the major works of each man respectively. But my books are not identical to one another. Their differences reflect differences in the style, thought, and problems which each man faced in the elaboration of his psychology. We will consider those differences at length below.

Because their lives were so intertwined and because their joint and individual labors have influenced modern thought so deeply, Freud's and Jung's relationship to one another is of profound interest. Freud and Jung realized this. Their letters to each other and interpretative works by contemporary scholars explore these issues in depth. I refer to many of these works in the appendix.

It is misleading to consider Jung only within the context of his relationship to Freud. His training, orientations, and ideals were distinctly unlike those of Freud. The major goal of this book is to suggest a way to read and understand Jung in his uniqueness and as he wished to be understood. In other words, I take him at face value and ask what did he say and was it coherent?

Jung the Man and Jung the Scientist

Carl Gustav Jung was a famous scientist and a famous personality. He was born in 1875 in Switzerland. He died there in 1961. Trained in psychiatry, he published important works as early as 1902. In 1909 Clark University in Worcester, Massachusetts, honored him and Sigmund Freud when it invited each man to deliver public lectures marking the twentieth anniversary of the opening of the university. Freud published his lectures as *Five Lectures on Psycho-Analysis* (SE 11, pp. 3-55). I discuss these lectures in the first chapter of my *Reading Freud*. Jung published his in various journals. In addition to these formal publications, both men wrote extensive analyses of what transpired between them on the boat trip to America. We consider Jung's account at length below when we read his *Memories, Dreams, Reflections*.

For some fifty years Jung wrote, taught, lectured, conducted work-shops and trained both physicians and lay persons in analytical psychol-ogy, the name given to his set of doctrines. In these endeavors Jung believed he was carrying out a scientific enterprise. Was he correct? We cannot answer this question without reading what he said and consider-ing it at length.

The question as to what constitutes "true science" is as contentious an issue in our day as what constituted "true religion" was in the Middle Ages. Not only are practicing scientists ready to offer definitions; a whole branch of modern philosophy has devoted itself to raising this issue to profound depths and, sometimes, plausible heights. When one raises the name of Jung or his school within hearing of many self-proclaimed "phi-losophers of science," one meets with a surprising amount of moralisms and denunciations of all Jung's errors, pretense, etc. These exhortations flourish typically in the midst of perfect innocence about what Jung actually said. Indeed, it requires no logical acumen to point out that the ready abuse and vitriol which so many academics are ready to loose upon the very name of Jung is entirely irrational.

This is so for two reasons. First, as noted, most of his attackers know little or nothing about his work. Second, Jung's general theory is expli-citly rationalistic. Our initial readings in his experimental papers will verify this claim. Then why do otherwise cautious academics and literati who would not dare trespass upon the methodological boundaries of their colleagues, without express written consent, plunge into denuncia-tions of Jung? Perhaps they are defending the honor of the enlighten-ment tradition of rational exploration against Jung's "obvious" penchant for irrational ideas, mysticism, and the black tide of the occult? Again, this cannot be true, it seems to me, because a fair reading of Jung does not demonstrate anything like this. Yet surely there is something a little suspect about a man who spent a good part of his life talking with schizophrenics, reading Latin texts on medieval alchemy, and most damning, reporting his visions?

On the other side of the question, one might suppose that Jung's friends, supporters, and students would rally behind his claim to scien-tific method and scientific discovery. For surely they read him as he wished to be read? Surely they would take him at face value? Yes, some have. But in my readings, and more so in my discussions and teaching, the majority of persons who identify themselves as "Jungian" do not. Many who find themselves attracted to Jung's thought, particularly reli-gionists, side with the majority of academics who denounce Jung's claim to scientific merit. Both groups see Jung as a modern prophet, a kind of secular, psychological saint, a guide to a way of knowing, and a keeper of particularly mysterious secrets. The academic scoffers reject out of hand the possibility of such a person; the faithful, self-identified Jungians accept it and celebrate it. I believe both groups are wrong because they identify incorrectly Jung's basic goals and his basic methods.

Before describing those goals and methods, the reader new to Jung might perform a small thought-experiment. Jung was keenly aware of the worldwide interest in UFOs in the 1950s and 1960s. How would he evaluate such phenomena? As signs of the second coming? As verifications of the universal truths of archaic religion? As mass psychosis? These questions are analogous to: Did Jung believe in God? Did he have special revelations? Or, can we use his insights to justify and support, if not validate, the faith claims of a particular religion? We will read his responses to all these questions. For the moment, it may prove useful to report that a large number of his students and the general public were quite sure the answer to them all was "yes." Hence an entirely mistaken and distorted report that Jung "believed in flying saucers" made world-wide headlines. Jung's clear and vigorous protest and his clarification were lost upon the general public. Jung reflected upon this systematic distortion. We consider his thought upon it below as well.

There is a substantial body of fine scholarly work on Jung; I try to identify it in the appendix to this book. I only wish to suggest how peculiar is our common task: to read Jung as he wished to be read. Indeed, one might say that our task is to read him in the "phenomenological" manner he treated himself and his patients. This brings us, again, to the question of his goals and methods.

Jung's Goals and Methods

It is more accurate to say "some" of Jung's goals and methods. As mentioned above, we do not read everything he wrote; nor do we read his major and influential works on the theory of psychological types, and on schizophrenia. We read Jung as a scientist who carried out a general research program. That program consisted in accounting for the appearance and persistence of human behaviors which were contrary to norms of rationalist metaphysics and rationalist psychologies. No one can doubt there are numerous instances of such behavior: from beliefs in ghosts, palm reading, and numerology, to the more rarified forms like Christian theology. These behaviors exist; they have existed from the beginnings of recorded history. Their popularity, importance, and roles in the daily life of innumerable people have not yielded to some three-hundred years of rationalist attack. Jung recognized this. His question was, in much simplified form, why? Why do they persist? Note that this is not identical to asking, "Are such beliefs true?". The latter question asks one to decide either for or against the believers.

To answer it is to take a side in the great battle between adamant believers and adamant critics of religion and other forms of non-rational belief and allegiance. Jung sided with neither group; he never answered the question of "belief" versus "unbelief." One might see this as cowardice; if he valued religion so highly, why not come clean and take part in one of its confessions, like Catholicism? Jung was an extremely protean personality; one might find within his rich and diverse writings, and his even richer and more divergent life, elements of cowardice. But again, our goal is not to psychoanalyze Jung. (From the period when he and Freud spent a great deal of their individual genius upon that task there has been a surplus of interpretations of Jung's personality.) Our task is to identify the core research problem Jung assigned himself and to isolate, through a systematic questioning, the solutions he advanced. No doubt Jung's background, his inner experiences, particularly as described in his autobiographical account, *Memories, Dreams, Reflections* (1961), his relationship to Freud, and other events shaped his work. But those external forces, like his relationship to Freud, no longer exist. They are fascinating and perhaps crucial elements of the history of ideas. They are not part of his *Collected Works*. And it is those sets of volumes with which we are concerned. Identifying that research program and selecting the texts which will best represent it is not easy.

Texts and References Used

Jung wrote a great deal, revised what he wrote, and had numerous translations made of his German pieces, the large majority of his writings through the sixty years he composed. Most scholarly readers will refer to the texts established in the *Collected Works of C. G. Jung* (20 volumes, 1953–1979, Princeton: Princeton University Press), hereafter referred to as CW. (His autobiography is hereafter referred to as MDR.)

There are problems with relying solely upon the CW. Unlike Freud, Jung wrote both technical and highly popular works, the latter predominating in his later years. These popular works have, naturally, appealed to most people, including most non-Jungian scholars. They form the bulk of the CW's eighteen volumes of text. Yet they are often repetitions and sometimes exact replications of his earlier, more technical works. It is these earlier, more technical works which we read. One can read his other texts with more leisure and less work.

A more serious problem is that the CW translates and, as it were, hallows Jung's late editions, usually subsuming the content and argument of the earlier editions to footnotes, or nothingness. Homans (1979) has sounded this complaint loudly and well when he noted that one could not rely upon the CW to represent either (1) Jung's works in a chronological sequence, or (2) their original form. These are crucial deficiencies when one wishes to see what Jung said, for example, in his works of 1908–1914 when he split with Freud. Homans notes that in the first edition of *Wandlungen und Symbole der Libido*, published in 1912 as *Psychology of the Unconscious*, Jung's struggle with Freud was direct and obvious. By the time Jung revised the book a fourth time those elements had disappeared; it is that fourth edition which appears as volume five in the CW as *Symbols of Transformation*. This frustrates the teacher who wishes to present Jung's work diachronically in the belief that, like most thinkers, Jung developed his ideas over time and along specific axes. (One can rely upon CW 19, which does list all his works in strict chronology.) It also forces us to read Jung more synchronically than we might wish. This has a peculiarly Jungian feeling to it; reading is a paradigmatic exercise in linear, diachronic, activity. One reads left to right, top to bottom, and from page to page. One *cannot* read any other way. Yet is that the only way the human mind can grasp meaning? Perhaps we are too idolatrous of diachronic explications and explanations in general?

Causal explanations are always diachronic since the cause always precedes the effect. Might there be alternative, non-linear modes of grasping meaning and insight? Are not some experiences of vision, creativity, and the like whole and complete in themselves at a single moment in time? Perhaps Jung's continuous meddling with his texts signifies his struggle to represent a synchronic (and mythical) view of human life within the constraints of a diachronic and rationalistic medium? We see Jung himself contemplate this question in one of his major essays, "On Synchronicity," with which we wrestle in chapter four of this book.

How to Use This Book

One cannot read all of Jung at once. Hence I have structured this handbook or guide as if all its readers were intelligent generalists who have come upon Jung for the first time. Since my goal is to read Jung as closely as possible to the way he wished to be read, I follow his central arguments closely and systematically. I use a question-sheet format. I have used this format with some success in teaching aspects of Jung's thought. I believe it permits students enough structure to get them on the road; but does not prejudice their responses—except to the unavoidable degree that all interrogations presume some point of view. I begin the discussion of each new text with a listing of technical terms which will appear in it. Since Jung altered and expanded the meaning of many such terms, they may appear more than once in my listing. See the index for a complete reference to each occurrence.

For someone working alone I hope this text might act like a friendly tutor or fellow traveler who has learned a bit about the local landscape and can help one get started.

All Freud references are to *The Standard Edition of the Complete Psychological Works of Sigmund Freud*, edited by James Strachey, London: The Hogarth Press, the twenty-fourth and last volume of which was published in 1966, hereafter referred to as SE followed by volume and page numbers.

I

JUNG'S EARLY PERIOD: PSYCHIATRIC STUDIES

On the Psychology and Pathology of So-Called Occult Phenomena (1902) CW 1

"On Hysterical Misreading" (1904), "Cryptomnesia" (1905) CW 1

"Experimental Researches" (1904–1907) CW 2

"The Associations of Normal Subjects" (1904) CW 2

"Psychoanalysis and Association Experiments" (1906) CW 2

"Association, Dream, and Hysterical Symptom" (1906) CW 2

We may identify two distinct trains of thought in Jung's early works: one is the investigation of the occult and paranormal. The other is the creation of a scientific method suitable to these investigations. We see both trains of thought emerge in his first major work: his medical dissertation, *On the Psychology and Pathology of So-Called Occult Phenomena* (CW 1) published in 1902. Although it is only some eighty pages long, his dissertation reflects the attitudes and feelings he had about the occult throughout his life.

Introduction

Technical Terms

Double consciousness; neurasthenia; epileptoid; twilight states; somnambulism; anamnesis; automatisms; unconscious personalities; feeling-toned ideas; cryptomnesia; autonomous ego-complex; teleological significance.

1. The CW editors have divided up this short work into four major sections. We follow them roughly in this common reading. Consider the terms Jung lists in the first paragraph: are these external descriptions or are they self-reports? That is, on what grounds would one say that a certain behavior was an instance of "double consciousness" versus "somnambulism"?

2. What makes answering this question and similar ones about the precise nature of psychopathology in general so difficult? Does our difficulty in carrying out such definitions give us any hints as to the likely origins and source of the immense variety of both

"occult" and normal behavior? That is, do we meet identical problems in the classification of strictly organic diseases?

3. Jung advances the case of Miss E (pp. 5–9). Which elements of
her life appear responsible for the outbreak of symptoms? From
what sources might she have derived the content of her hallucinations? For example, why might her visions of skeletons, etc.,
appear between midnight and 1:00 A.M. in the night (p. 7)?

4. Jung seems concerned to establish whether or not such patients
can recall the exact content of their hallucinations and delusions
once they are "cured" or at least healthy. Why? Why does their
general inability to connect the two argue in favor of a hypothesis
of a "second state" with a memory of its own (p. 9)?

5. After discussing similar cases, Jung says Miss E exhibited "Inci-
dental auto-suggestions" (p. 13). What kind of term is this? How
does it fit in Jung's basic concern in this section? Why does he
invoke the name and example of Goethe, the great German poet
and scientist, when discussing the range and variety of such
altered states of consciousness? If Jung is correct ought everyone
to report similar, if not as dramatic, instances from their own
experience?

6. Jung sums up the case of Miss E and offers what appears to be an
explanation on p. 16. Is it a full explanation? Does he suggest it
lacks anything in the way of completeness? He uses the case of
Miss E to lead into his presentation of his own patient, Miss SW.
What goals does he have for his presentation? Will it offer a final
explanation of hallucinations and visionary experiences?

7. He begins part II, the description of the case, with a note that he
knew the girl and a note on his method. What kinds of details can
we guess he omitted from his record of the girl's "romances"?
Does one find Freud omitting similar details in his case histories?
Why not?

8. Jung describes her (and his) family background, then her particular "normal" characteristics. Why does he emphasize that she was
especially mediocre in most of her doings and that she had no
recourse to mystical books of any kind? How should we characterize her parents and consequently the quality of her life with
them? Can we reconstruct the general way she probably understood her life and her surroundings?

9. Jung describes her as an excellent medium and her effect upon
her audience as "astonishing." About what sorts of things is one
astonished? Consider two or three examples of astonishing events
and then attempt to reconstruct what gives them their common
tone? Why is a demonstration of extrasensory perception astonishing, while high-speed typewriters, for example, are not?

10. Why does he describe her state as somnambulistic? And why is he, with the others, convinced of its authenticity? Note: Is Jung agreeing with the content of her spirit messages when he calls these "experiments"? Why does he point out how in these states her movements were fine and of a noble grace?

11. "Her indignation was not faked" (p. 21). Why is this claim crucial to Jung's entire presentation of the case up to this point? In the same way, he is keen to record her color, always noting if it is extremely pale and waxen, just as he notes her breathing and other physiological responses. Why are these manifestations so important to his reconstruction of the case?

12. Does Jung doubt her story, at least in these initial reports? What elements in her behavior appear to support the claim that she is not faking her visions? For example, does Jung believe her when she reports a terrifying vision of a copper-red face (p. 22)? Just as her initial pronouncements astonished her family, Jung says he was amazed by her calmness in accepting her new-found role as a seer and medium. Shortly afterwards, her sisters also hallucinate; are they faking their responses? Jung does not appear to believe this is true; does that mean he accepts their own self-interpretations?

13. "Her solemn behaviour had something sorrowful and melancholy about it. She was painfully conscious of the great difference between her nocturnal ideal world and the crude reality of day" (p. 24). Why does Jung invoke these aesthetic judgments at this point? How might we understand his claim that it was in these moods she produced her best results? Using what criteria does he arrive at this judgment?

14. Jung reports SW was very adept at receiving messages (p. 25). What does this mean? Note, she *cannot* receive from other mediums, whom one would expect to be among the best "senders." Assuming Jung is correct, can SW's spiritual theory of her talents—that she but said what they told her—be correct? How could laying one's hand on the table give her any clues as to one's question, much less the correct answer? (Note that her interrogators did not verbalize their questions; but they had to touch her or the table, "Direct thought transference could never be established" (p. 25.) Therefore how was the question communicated to her?)

15. The "Records of the Seances" reports SW's method in detail. Consider the "psychograph" (p. 25); are there similar items in our ordinary experience? When one is distraught what kinds of signs or signals or other messages might one seek? Consider how many daisies and other petaled flowers get pulled apart; in what kind of mood must one be in order to entertain such beliefs? Do most people believe such things at some part of their life?

16. Immediately after the fourth setting SW read a book about a similar medium who used "magnetism" to increase and deepen her communications with the spirits. Why is Jung not concerned about the obvious degree to which SW adapted herself to this new knowledge? If Jung were himself seeking after a real contact with the "spirit world," would he be so nonchalant about this interference with SW's purity?

17. In reporting these episodes Jung is keenly aware of SW's physical state. Why does he call these earliest episodes *attacks* of somnambulism? Soon we meet two characters: her grandfather and Ulrich von Gerbenstein. Why does Jung make a point of assessing the aesthetic qualities, as it were, of each? Does Ulrich know what SW knows and does she know what he knows, or says and does when he dominates the seances? How should we understand Jung's remark that the control spirit, SW's grandfather, is quite unlike the "historical reality" (p. 31)?

18. Paragraph 58 is particularly important to Jung's exposition. What is the medium's "somnambulistic" ego (p. 32)? Given Jung's claims about the portions of the seances which are *not* available to SW, which portions of her personality are inferior and which superior to her ordinary, waking ego? When she is awakened she cannot recall the automatic phenomena; she can recall her loud talking. Can we arrange these facts into some kind of hierarchical order as well?

19. We finally come to her description of her somnambulistic ego (pp. 33–34). This personage describes many marvelous things about Mars, the afterlife, the spirit world, and so forth. Why does she not convey information about ordinary life and help us solve ordinary problems? Consider the spell she cast upon Conventi, on p. 35; without knowing the language in which it is written which of its characteristics are "spell-like"? (Cf. spells uttered by some of Shakespeare's characters.)

20. Jung reports that SW, upon learning of the Clairvoyante of Prevorst, hinted at her own extraordinary family tree. While her "romance" is vivid and spectacular in parts, why does Jung not challenge her on some point of logic or history? Why, in other words, does he not attempt to verify the possibility of her stories being false? How might we understand her claims to be related to Goethe, and the mother to both her father and her grandfather? What is their source and what characterizes their composition?

21. In the "mystic science" section, Jung describes SW's detailed map of the spiritual realm (p. 40). He mentions one possible source of some of these ideas, but he does not pursue the question further. Why not? What appears to be the internal logic of the seven

circles and the various powers? Given the presence of "dark powers," why are we not surprised to come upon "light powers" as
well? Where else does one find this kind of dualistic thinking?

22. The termination of the authentic seances is as puzzling as their
    initial appearance. What features of the terminal seances, just
    prior to her faking, suggested SW had lost her authenticity? Had
    she lost her talent? Had she faked everything? How should we
    understand the fact that her power decreased following her de-
    scription of the seven realms? Are these two facts causally related?
    And are they related to the improvements in her character?

23. In his discussion of the case Jung presents a physiological explana-
    tion of SW's major symptoms. How are disturbances in attention
    related to the elementary automatic phenomena SW exhibited in
    her early seances? How are these, in turn, related to her "psychic
    shadow side"? And how does Jung explain the fact that as SW
    advanced in her psychic performances the rudimentary automa-
    tisms disappeared? What view or model of the human mind is
    implied in Jung's use of the term *surface of consciousness*?

24. Jung answers this latter question at length when he describes the
    characteristics of semi-somnambulism and the automatisms, includ-
    ing hallucinations, SW manifested. Why must Jung argue that there
    are intimate, unconscious connections between the motor and
    speech areas of the brain? What perceptual skills would tend to
    characterize successful mediums? (Note p. 49, note 32.)

25. "One can see . . . how the unconscious personality builds itself up"
    (p. 53). Does that mean we can conclude nothing about the
    "depths" of a personality by assessing the kind of unconscious
    personalities it constructs in such circumstances? If such construc-
    tion helped SW, or at least issued in a much improved level of
    functioning, might it constitute a form of psychotherapy? And if
    it is a form of psychotherapy and if it has similarities to other
    "mystical sciences," how should medical science assess the latter?

26. In different circumstances SW's behavior and her claims to mysti-
    cal knowledge might be subsumed under a medical category of
    extreme mental illness, for example, paranoid psychosis. Jung does
    not avoid making these kinds of diagnoses, but he does not pursue
    them either. On the contrary, he invokes comparisons with
    Freud's theory of repressions in dreams (pp. 56–57). How does
    this comparison in fact "normalize" SW's actions? If the aim of
    psychological treatment is to uncover the repressed, how does the
    emergence of sub-personalities contribute to therapeutic aims?

27. Jung attempts to explain why SW had visual, rather than auditory
    hallucinations, and why so many diverse persons, including Spi-
    noza, experience similar visions in altered states of consciousness,

especially just prior to sleeping. With many other scientists of his day he explains such hallucinations as due to environmental and physical sensations. But those who hallucinate do not share this opinion; why do they pursue personalistic and spiritual explanations? What makes the latter so much more attractive than Jung's physiological accounts?

28. Where among the range of types Jung presents ought we to place SW's second personality, Ivenes? Is she completely unlike a pathological liar, or a dreamer, or a psychotic, or even a very good actress who portrays her role vividly and with deep feeling? Where else and in what occupations or historical roles do we find persons who claim extraordinary abilities to communicate with the "spirits" or to see the future? Are they always judged insane? And were they? (This question takes on special importance when we read Jung's autobiographical account.)

29. Among Jung's central concepts, that of archetype is particularly rich and, consequently, subject to numerous interpretations and condemnations. Before considering it in its developed sense it will prove useful to list and rank the varieties of other-than self psychological constellations. For example, rank and compare Freud's notion of "unconscious train of thought" (p. 69, note 90), Binet's notion of "parasitic intelligences" (p. 69), and Jung's notion of "feeling-toned ideas" (p. 68). Are they merely different names for the same phenomenon? Why does Freud stress the claim that ideas and feelings subject to a drop in attention cathexis are those which will not bear criticism? Are SW's romances and thoughts of this nature?

30. Jung then attempts to explain what caused the somnambulistic attacks. Under psychic excitation he describes moments of intense feeling. Are all his examples of a single, affective kind? That is, is the "witch's sleep" identical to the episode from the Flaubert novel or to the account of Betina Brentano and Goethe? The latter two examples would seem to be illustrations of intense pleasure which, somehow, brought about swooning. But is swooning characteristic of all intense psychological pleasures? If not, do Jung's examples share a deeper, common affective root?

31. The discussion of SW's many partial personalities is confusing. For example, Jung speaks of them as if they were independent persons and as if they were but aspects of the young girl's total personality. Which are they? He reports that all the spirits who emerge during the seances can be reduced to two types. What are those two types and how is each related to the other? That is, what formal qualities does each share with the other? Ought we expect to find a similar set in the unconscious of all persons?

32. Jung attempts to clarify the situation on pp. 74–76 where he describes the process by which an automaticism gives rise to somnambulistic phenomena (note that he distinguishes between the visionary state, dreaming, hallucinatory states and somnambulistic attacks). Why does Jung say that the Grandfather figure functions like Ivenes's hypnotist (p. 77)? Does Jung himself believe the patient is "split" entirely into two personalities?

33. What is the "truest and most original property of the 'supraconscious' personality" (p. 77)? Given this property how ought we to understand the numerous conflicts that emerge between SW's subpersonalities? What is their aim? Should medical specialists attempt to prevent their appearance in persons like SW? Are there non-medical environments or institutions in which people like SW might function without incurring social disapproval?

34. Jung summarizes his description of the unconscious personalities; one class he ascribes to the dream ego, another to the automata (pp. 77–78). How does he himself judge both groups? Is either to be preferred over the other? How do such somnambulistic personalities represent a "teleological significance" (p. 79)? Again, considering this teleological dimension of SW's symptoms, how should psychotherapists intervene when similar symptoms appear in their patients' behaviors?

35. True to his overall concerns Jung attempts to account for heightened unconscious performance by way of physiological considerations. If what Binet reports is correct, or roughly so, what must we conclude about the ordinary person's belief that psychological existence is exhausted by conscious experiencing? If Jung is correct in his summary of the evidence he and other authorities present, where, as it were, must we locate in the psychic economy skills that require insight and creativity? And given that, how would most persons who are creative understand the source of their gift? (Why might they be particularly superstitious?) Why does Nietzsche say one ought not to ask from whom one's insight comes?

36. In his "Conclusions" Jung raises a question which will emerge numerous times in his subsequent explorations: Why do we find that the psychotic-like products of a young girl's two-year fling with the occult are so strikingly similar to the products of religious and philosophical systems of which she had no direct knowledge? The Gnostics were members of religious sects whom the early and medieval Christian church sought to obliterate. Why would gnostic-like beliefs emerge in the adolescent drama Jung describes in this monograph?

37. We learn from MDR that SW died of tuberculosis when she was age twenty-six. Before her death she regressed to the condition of

a two-year-old. Should this fact count against Jung's psychological explanations of her visions?

"On Hysterical Misreading" (1904); "Cryptomnesia" (1905) CW 1

1. These two short papers are expansions of some of Jung's remarks in his dissertation. In the first paper he distinguishes between ordinary errors of misreading and hysterical ones. What is the difference? How does he distinguish the "formal" from the "sense" connection?

2. One sometimes reads that Jung believed there was a three-story structure to the mind: the conscious level being the uppermost and under it a personal unconscious and under that the collective unconscious. Why is this an incomplete understanding of his model of the mind? How does he explain a hysteric woman's ability to read a text, understand it, but remain incapable of saying what she read?

3. In "Cryptomnesia" Jung sets out crucial ideas in a deceptively simple way. We saw how SW was able to perceive messages sent her by subliminal routes, e.g., the table tappings, from other members of the seance. She was extraordinary; do ordinary people have similar skills? Do most people agree that all psychic processes are "strictly determined" (p. 96)? Jung had read Freud's major contributions to the question of overdetermination (his *Interpretation of Dreams* [1900]). If they are both correct, why can a psychologist presume to reconstruct the "feeling-toned complex" simply on the basis of a song or a few associations?

4. This short piece is about the technical term "cryptomnesia." How does Jung connect it to the much broader issues of creativity, genius, psychopathology, and the labor by which Nature "builds laboriously on what has gone before" (p. 101)? What is Jung's evaluation of the depths of the psyche? What is the tone of his warnings to those who do not exercise continually the most rigorous self-criticism (p. 99)?

5. "Only this elemental force can wrench from oblivion the oldest and most delicate traces in a man's memory . . ." (p. 105). What is this force? For those who know Freud's works, do you find anything similar in his evaluation of the unconscious? Is Jung saying in this text that one might have access to delicate traces of thought derived from *previous* generations? Are his claims incompatible with that hypothesis?

Jung's next major contribution to psychiatry was his series of papers on the Word Association Test which he helped refine during his work at the Burgholzi Mental Hospital in Zurich.

"Experimental Researches" (1904–1907) CW 2
"The Associations of Normal Subjects," with Franz Riklin (1904) CW 2

Technical terms

Association; stimulus word; constellation; feeling-toned complex; reaction-types; internal and external distractions; "A-phenomenon"; habituation; preseveration; attitude phenomena; repression; affect.

1. Jung's reputation is generally that of a mystical sort of softheaded religious philosopher who deviated from Freud's teachings and, if one is contra-Freud, transcended his teacher or, if one is pro-Freud, abandoned the true faith. Does either of these assessments match the tone and concerns of this text's introductory comments? What is Jung's rationale for replicating many features of his director's previous studies of the process of word association? Is this a deductive or inductive approach to the question?

2. Jung says the process of association is immensely complex and "subject to countless psychic events, which cannot be objectively established" (p. 4). If this is so, what use is it to conduct word association tests? Why must he (and his co-author) emphasize the centrality of *attention* to the process? Is attention itself a simple process? Can one hope to give a complete account of something which is an "infinitely complicated mechanism" (p. 4)? (On all these issues see Howard C. Warren, *A History of Association Psychology* [New York: Scribner's Sons, 1921] and R. MacKinnon and W. F. Dukes, "Repression" in *Psychology in the Making*, ed. Leo Postman [New York: Knopf, 1962, pp. 662–744].)

3. The authors summarize their two major questions: do they confine them to psychiatry alone or to the explanation of psychopathology alone? The first question—what are the laws—seems straightforward. The second is more obscure: what is the "valency of the associations"? And what is the "focus of consciousness"? Have we seen these two concepts operating already in Jung's study of SW?

Part I. General Experimental Procedure

4. After describing the number and types of normal subjects, Jung reports that he and Riklin "naturally" administered the test to one another. Why "naturally"? Why could each not administer it to himself? If you have not taken such tests, nor read much about them, what tone or atmosphere would appear to dominate the testing situation? In fact, would the testers prefer their subjects to know the scientific literature well or would they prefer their subjects to be as naive as possible? Why might deceit and trickery

become typical features of psychological testing and experimentation in our time? How do you account for the "schoolroom" attitude (p. 7) which many of the uneducated subjects had toward the test?

5. Is this related to their paradoxical struggle with responding stimulus words uttered in their native dialect? Jung says the uneducated Swiss is not accustomed to experiencing (hearing?) words individually, but only in acoustic-motor connection with other words. Is this plausible? Would this mean they have no interest in puns, word-plays, jokes and other linguistic games which focus on individual words?

6. The WAT has three parts. The first entails 200 stimulus words and reactions. The second and third are more complicated. In them the authors attempted to interfere with their subjects' normal ability to attend to the aural stimulus (the stimulus word as it was spoken by the experimenter). Jung's exposition is a little too condensed here since the majority of his readers will not know what the "A-phenomenon" is, nor what "internal distractions" might be. He illustrates both on pp. 40 and 47. At this juncture we note that only educated persons could undergo this series of experiments: why?

7. The investigation of associations precedes Jung by many centuries. Both philosophers and experimental psychologists, especially those whom Wilhelm Wundt influenced, asserted they would found a scientific psychology by focusing upon the primary units of experience: associations. Upon what basic assumptions about human nature and about the primary units or substances of nature do these beliefs rest? That is, where, as it were, do these investigators locate the core or essential items of human experience?

8. Jung tells us all his subjects were required to complete a third experimental sequence: this using external distractions. Both educated and uneducated persons had to keep time to a metronome as they responded to the stimulus words. Why do the experimenters add this third sequence? Have we seen similar kinds of distraction in the account of SW? Did she in effect rely upon external distractions when she induced her altered states? (Did her "internal hypnotist" carry out similar kinds of distraction?)

9. Jung adds a fourth class of subjects: those who took the test while they were severely fatigued. Again, have we seen SW engaged in similar experiments with herself? Why might some creative persons find they work best when they are a little drowsy, or have their best ideas upon awakening or just before falling asleep? (This latter question will reappear when we read MDR and consider Jung's own creative habits and style.)

Part II. Classification

10. Jung's discussion of the association may appear a little paradoxical; does he believe there are actual physical or neurological linkages between words in the brain which the WAT elicits? If not, how should one understand the behavior which the test evokes? And why must we, again, distinguish the quality of associations by educated persons from the quality of those by uneducated persons?

11. If the WAT does not uncover an actual, neurological linkage, between the stimulus word and the subject's response, what is it evoking? Does the test permit us to make any claims about the subject's internal life? (Does Jung believe his tests have established empirical laws? If not, what additional data does he require?) For example, how does the test permit one to say a patient exhibits a "flight of ideas"?

12. Jung sets out the logic of his classification scheme on p. 14 (CW 2). He summarizes it on pp. 36–39. His lettering scheme is confusing; note he has four main categories of types of associations (categories A, B, C, and D) and four characteristic types of response (categories E, F, G, and H). It will pay us to examine the criteria by which he assigns particular responses to each major category. (The WAT is easy to simulate; why not give it to a friend and vice-versa?)

13. Note the first two categories appear to be contraries of one another: how does Jung distinguish internal from external associations? Are the subcategories of internal association based purely upon semantic grounds? Before considering the subcategories of internal associations, compare the length of Jung's description of the entire category with those of the second, third, and fourth categories. What do these relative lengths tell us about the relative weight Jung (or his subjects) gives to "internal" connections?

14. It will prove useful to give your own examples for each subcategory, e.g., give an example of "co-ordination" (p. 15); of "subordination" (p. 17); of "superordination" (pp. 17–18); and of "contrast" (pp. 18–19). What must one know of the stimulus words in order to claim, as Jung does, that the response fits into any one of these four categories? That is, could one make these assignments using a standard dictionary? Consider the pairs "father–uncle" and "father–God" (from p. 16). Does Webster's make these connections in the definition of the term *father*? If not, what kind of knowledge do these pairings require? (Are there any reference books which would help one investigate such pairings?) Note the same issues for the examples of "contrast": what kind of reference aid would serve one in this case?

15. The second major subcategory of internal associations is predication (pp. 19–24). Why is the association "snake–green" entirely synthetic? What is an example of a purely analytic association? Why is a synthetic judgment "in a way superior to the analytic" (p. 20)? Of the two kinds of judgment, which appears the easier to make? Would uneducated persons grasp this distinction very quickly? Would *all* experimenters agree with each of Jung's classifications? (Is there room for disagreement?)

16. After summarizing the four types of predicative responses, the first two of which have subcategories, Jung mentions "causal relationships" (p. 24). This category is astonishingly brief: stimulus word and reaction [response word] are linked by a causal connection. Why is this category so simple while the one above it was so complex?

17. Moving on to the second major category, External Associations, Jung again describes a series of complex subcategories. What is the major distinction between internal and external types? Note under "linguistic-motor forms" (p. 25) he lists pairs of terms which appear like those we saw under the category of "contrast" (Internal Associations), e.g., "dark–light." How does their having been "cannalized" by use justify Jung's decision to place them in the category of external associations? Would one expect especially intelligent people to have more or fewer internal associations than the norm?

18. In the third major category, Sound Reactions, Jung lists responses which appear to be "caused" by the mere acoustic pattern of the term, e.g., word completion, similar sounding words, and rhymes. We note that this list is also very short and, when compared to the subtleties of the first category, defined simply. Does it follow that people who give a large number of sound-association responses are either less educated or less intelligent than those who give fewer? Under what conditions do you find yourself or other persons responding to their environment with these kind of associations? (Cf. "clang-associations" in descriptive psychiatry.)

19. Under the fourth and last major category, "Miscellaneous," Jung lists what may appear to be trivial examples since they did not fit his and Riklin's schema (p. 28). But are they trivial kinds of responses? Of the four subcategories Jung describes (indirect association; meaningless reactions; failures; and repetition), which are tied intimately to "feeling-toned" complexes? In which kind of persons would we therefore expect to find them predominate?

20. The last four major categories (E, F, G, and H in Jung's schema) describe characteristic types of responses. Who is most likely to give these kinds of responses? That is, what kind of subjects

exhibit ego-centricisms, preseveration, repetitions, and solely motor-acoustic associations? Given Jung's assessment, what can we predict about the likelihood of intelligent, well-educated, and healthy subjects exhibiting any of these forms of association?

III. Results of the Experiment

Technical Terms

Reaction type; blunting of reaction type; the unconscious; repressed; return of the repressed; attitude phenomenon.

1. Jung tells us again that even his educated subjects found it difficult to produce and respond to "internal distractions" (p. 40). These are produced by people who have the ability to observe the internal processes by which they produce an association at the same time they respond verbally. For example, to the stimulus word "train" an educated person may note that she imagines immediately a locomotive engine upon which is a white veil ("wedding train") and hears herself utter the association "engine." Jung asked his subjects to pay attention to this element in their response as they reacted to the stimulus word. Since this takes extra effort, he labeled it an internal distraction. (See "free-association" in Freud and in the index to CW 2.)

2. From p. 40 to p. 135 Jung summarizes the scores of thirty-eight subjects, arranged into four classes (educated and uneducated and by sex). Unlike other experimenters who employ the association test, Jung and his co-worker are especially interested in the performance of individuals under stress. Why? Why not confine the experiment to normal and healthy persons alone? How does he hope to use his findings to amplify the scientific understanding of psychopathology? Does he view the very sick person as wholly unlike the normal?

3. If we discover that the frequency of one type of response increases with fatigue or emotional tension or under either internal or external distraction, what can we generalize about its appearance in normals? (Cf. Jung's discussion of the increase in failures, preserverations, and sound associations in the first set of subjects, educated women [pp. 40–70].)

4. At the same time, Jung says he can type each subject according to her characteristic form of response, e.g., p. 65. Assuming his results are repeatable and coherent, does it follow that his subjects would agree with his claims about their "type"? That is, is he measuring "unconscious" characteristics as well as conscious ones? Is there a genetic basis to these distinct types? Why does the fact

that a woman's daughter shows a "blunter reaction type" require urgent attention and investigation (p. 66)? How should we account for the fact that distraction failed in four of the definite predicate types and was less pronounced in all subjects who manifested a predicate typology?

5. Turning to the male subjects, Jung says he measured their performance under different states of disturbed attention. Why does he find fatigue states so interesting? Reactions of sleeping persons to the stimulus word would be entirely based on sound associations (p. 72). Why? If this is true, what should we expect to find when sleeping persons hear spoken language? And in general what change in sound reactions should we see as fatigue and external distraction increase in severity?

6. Blunt reaction types (p. 73) exhibit a sharp distinction in their responses; why do persons who suffer from emotionally charged complexes (p. 72) do the same? The patient described on these pages exhibited finally sound reactions alone. Why? And what kind of responses would typify SW's responses as she entered her somnambulent state?

7. How does the presence of strong repression (a term Jung adopted from Freud and Breuer [1895]) alter a subject's normal responses? If Jung is correct, could one use the WAT to assess a patient's need for or capacity to use psychological treatment? In this important passage Jung describes both "constellations" and "feeling-toned-complexes" (pp. 78–82). What distinguishes the two? How does a severe complex lead to the formation of a large number of constellations? How else is the term constellation used in ordinary discourse? What psychological factors permitted the Greeks to find in the starry sky representations of gods and heroes? Why can we not see the same patterns, unless we are trained explicitly to do so?

8. Note Jung's language: the "constellation also expresses itself" (p. 83) and "Thus the complex makes use of a mode of reaction that is not unusual in this subject" (p. 87). Why does he grant a kind of activity to both kinds of psychic entities? To which portions of SW's behavior did Jung ascribe similar kinds of activity?

9. In complex-constellations the "reactions readily come in the form of sentences, in other associations only rarely" (p. 95). If this is true, what may we conclude about the genesis of the complex (or complex-constellation) itself? That is, was it ever in consciousness or under the direct control of the ego? (For those who have read Freud's *Interpretation of Dreams* [1900] compare this question to Freud's conception of the day-residue and the dream-wish.) Were SW's ideas and constructions coherent and expressed in complete sentences as well?

10. Yet Jung says that subjects need not be aware of the complexes which emerge and which, upon examination, are revealed in their associations (p. 101). Hence he says the complex is typically unconscious. If this is so, and if it can be shown by the WAT, what may we conclude about the validity of Freud's basic theorems on the ubiquity of repression? Why would lengthened reaction times, clang associations, and the emergence of non-typical reactions indicate the presence of such unconscious complexes?

Part IV. Uneducated Women

11. Jung's first case, number 24, is an excellent illustration of what he means by feeling-toned complex. Note that the number of complex-constellations decreases in the second part of the experiment. Why might this be so? Is it related to Jung's claims that naive subjects find the WAT extremely stimulating and, at first, exhibit strong affective responses to the test? Does the fact that they are of the lower classes responding to a superior physician influence their willingness to reveal themselves too?

12. Not all his subjects were so dramatic; his second example, on p. 108, exhibited a remarkable calmness. Why does Jung say she in effect masked the extent of her own complex-reactions? To what concepts in current ego-psychology should we assign these kinds of masking? Why does this woman, whom Jung says belongs to an objective reaction-type, respond with concepts like "good," and "well-behaved"? Are these merely "strict morals"? Why would she carry out the experiment with "great enthusiasm" and make great efforts (p. 112)?

13. Jung says some of his subjects, like number 26, responded to the stimulus words with reveries and rich daydreams. This particular nurse exhibits both in her dramatic responses. Is it fair to say she exhibits also a split or twofold quality in her consciousness? Is this similar to elements of CW's behavior when she was in the throes of her struggles?

14. Is one's reaction type fixed forever, never to change? If yes, how can we account for the fact that a complex well hidden behind a popular quotation permits one to give relatively quick reactions? How does a complete split in consciousness contribute to these apparent successes in hiding the complex? Does this permit us to account for SW's glibness and ease when she assumed the identity of her grandfather or Ulrich von Gerbenstein?

15. If religion incorporates basic themes of personal conflicts, ought the devout person to demonstrate a similar ease and lack of overt difficulties concerning these typical complexes?

16. In section IV, Uneducated Men, Jung says his subjects rarely exhibited any indications of the presence of complexes. Yet he reported many signs of the presence of complexes among his educated male subjects. The latter he says have "more feminine characteristics" (p. 136) than their uneducated brothers. If this is so how ought we to account for it? Is Jung's understanding of the reaction types based strictly upon a genetic hypothesis? That is, is one's reaction type determined by one's inherited characteristics alone? Do feminine men become educated more easily than non-feminine ones?

17. Does Jung answer this question directly in this text? We have raised this question above when we noted how the reactions and skills of educated subjects differed so markedly from those of the uneducated. How might the factor of "attention" help us reconceive these questions?

18. Jung gives a condensed description of the general notion of attention and its relationship to concentration. How does he account for the interesting fact that procedures like the WAT arouse numerous memories from childhood ? Are these memories merely forgotten, or suppressed, or repressed? With what kinds of behavior is the recollection of each type associated?

19. On pp. 140–146 he returns to the question of explaining why we find such striking differences between the reaction types found in educated males and those typical of uneducated males. He does not say the difference is due to fundamental differences in the genetic constitution of the two groups. Of the six factors he lists, what seems to typify the uneducated man's response to the experiment and to the experimenters? Why might the educated subjects be "lazier"?

20. Although Jung says people vary in their responses according to their perception of the experiment and their interpretation of what the experimenter wants from them, there emerge two distinct types: the subjective and the objective (pp. 148–149). What distinguishes the two types? Might one change from one to the other? If not, ought psychotherapy to aim at clarifying a patient's type and, as it were, allow it to emerge?

21. Alongside one's fundamental attitude are those associations governed by repressed or split-off complexes. What characterizes the experience of repression? When does one know that one is in fact struggling with a repressed idea? And when does one know one's subject is trying to keep the secret? Of the five major clues Jung lists on pp. 150–151, is any one of them *not* observable in normal persons at some time or another?

22. It would appear that there are major differences between male

and female reactions; does Jung agree? If the WAT does not show a consistent difference between the sexes, does that mean there is no difference? (Jung summarizes his response to this question in section III beginning on p. 163.) Why is he disappointed by the results of his experiments? If one found differences in associations determined by the subject's sex, what kind of causes could Jung then claim the WAT exhibited?

23. Does Jung grant any weight to the notion of randomness or psychical freedom? Are these two concepts identical? We will see him confront this question more directly in his autobiography and in his essays on psychopathology proper. (It is also related to the question of faking psychopathology: if one cannot fake a neurosis or insanity what shall we conclude about the degree to which actual neurotics are responsible for their disease?)

24. After describing the difference between predicate types under normal conditions with their behavior while under stress, Jung summarizes the major points of the study. Which factors are least predictive of reaction type and which most predictive? The second "Egocentric" attitude (or Subjective type) would appear to be more typical of neurotics since it includes the subcategory of the "constellation type." If this is correct does that mean one could use the WAT to diagnose the presence of neurosis in naive subjects?

Jung realized the importance of these questions and, contrary to the majority of psychologists, he employed the WAT precisely as a diagnostic tool. He also recognized the importance of explicating the grounds of a theory of psychological types. We consider his response to these questions in the papers which appear in CW 2, following this essay.

Shorter Pieces on the Association Method

Jung did an immense amount of work with the WAT. It was those studies which convinced him of the validity and importance of Freud's fundamental theories and which he presented to the senior man at their first meeting. Jung's use of (early) psychoanalytic methods is evident in two essays in CW 2, "Psychoanalysis and Association Experiments" and "Association, Dream, and Hysterical Symptom." In addition CW 2 contains translations of two short lectures Jung delivered at Clark University where he and Freud received honorary doctorates in 1909 for their individual and joint labors in psychoanalysis. Since the short essays are important but easy to read and the longer ones more difficult but also more important, we consider the latter below.

"Psychoanalysis and Association Experiments" (1906) CW 2

1. Jung summarizes Freud's major theorem about the genesis of hysterical symptoms: why is repression so central to that argument?
   If Freud is correct, could hysterics *ever* be able to state directly
   and coherently the meaning of their actions? Are all hysterics liars
   or something else?

2. After describing in brief Freud's method of free-association Jung
   says there is a second way of overcoming repression (that of the
   artists) plus a third way offered by the WAT. Why is the latter an
   especially convenient method? Why does the WAT call forth
   constellated complexes? Jung and others had used the test to fin-
   ger guilty persons suspected of crimes to which they would not
   confess. How does their success give them courage to apply it to
   neurotics?

3. He summarizes the case of Miss E on pp. 291–93. He gave her the
   WAT and then, independently of her associations, "diagnosed the
   complex." How and on what grounds was he able to do this? Could
   he have done so without the use of Freud's intervening theory? Are
   the associations of "table–woman" and "friendly–loving" always
   indicative of a repressed erotic complex?

4. How does the length of the reaction to "stranger" argue in favor
   of Jung's claim that his patient must have an extremely strong
   feeling about strangers and herself? Note too, the reaction
   "narrow–small" which Jung says is probably part of the body-
   complex (p. 300). To what kinds of knowledge must one have
   access in order to carry out this kind of detective work? For
   example, could non-German speaking persons guess that the
   response "still-stool" has erotic associations for this patient? (An
   excellent exercise to strengthen one's technique is to fabricate a
   WAT protocol for a fictional character, like Hamlet or Dr. Wat-
   son, and then ask one's colleagues to discover both the complexes
   and to whom they belong.)

5. On what further grounds does Jung say his patient has a complex
   which she has "every reason to repress" (p. 303)? It happens that
   his patient subsequently confirms these diagnoses, according to
   the way Jung writes this essay at least. Hence, Jung must have
   used some logical process by which he arrived at his conclusions.
   Why might a full and complete knowledge of sexual slang as well
   as dirty jokes and schoolyard biology serve the analyst well?

6. Having used the test and drawn his conclusions Jung confronts
   Miss E (p. 304). What are his tone and style in these confrontations? Would one expect to hear contemporary psychotherapists
   speak to their patients with equal vehemence, and to point out

their patients' "excuses and shiftings"? What keeps Jung steadfast in his beliefs and fires his determination to discover or uncover the repressed unconscious? (For those who have read Freud's case history of "Dora," "Fragment of an Analysis of a Case of Hysteria" [1909, SE 7] written around the same time as this, do you find a similar tone in the way Freud addresses his patient?)

7. In section 2, "Psychoanalysis," Jung records the need for absolute conviction in the face of neurotic protestations, and then gives us a detailed description of the first hour and a half session. Why did he push her back down into the chair, even if with "gentle force" (p. 305)? Does Miss E exhibit signs of repression or simply discomfort? She promises to do better in the second session but repeats the protests and interjections of the first. Is this repeated difficulty another sign of repression? Is her story coherent once it emerges?

8. Jung reports that she evinced the same kind of resistance in the third session but that her presentation was "matter of fact" (p. 308). How ought we to understand this interesting observation with the additional one that she reported these sexual histories and fantasies all the while muttering "I don't know" ? What elements of SW's reports were similar?

9. How much autonomy does Jung grant to the "split-off portions" of Miss E's personality? Explain what he means when he says, "Her everyday person and her sexual person are just two different complexes, two different aspects of consciousness that do not want to or must not know anything of one another" (p. 309). *Are* these identical to what Freud meant by repression? Do neurotics manifest a dual consciousness like Miss E's or like that of SW?

10. We return to this question when we consider Jung's second paper on a woman he diagnoses as "hysteric." Does Miss E appear to be someone whose difficulties are confined to sexual anxieties alone? Consider Jung's account of her love affair (p. 311). How realistic was she about this man and how insightful was she about the likelihood of his returning to her? Although we know nothing about him, how might a young man have responded to Miss E's general style? Would the young man have been surprised by Miss E's vigilant and constant yearning for him?

11. We read again of Miss E's difficulties with telling Jung her story, particularly about her intense sexual fantasies, masturbation, childhood sexual games with her sister. Are these elements also "repressed"? Jung says the patient "remembered every detail, frequently even the wording" (p. 312) of a sex book she read at the age of ten. Is this typical of hysterics?

12. Jung is surprised that Miss E avoided men and real sexual encounters "in spite of her sexually extraordinary lively fantasy" (p. 314).

Looking back with the benefit of eighty years of clinical advance, is Miss E's rejection of authentic sexuality surprising to us? This raises again the question of Miss E's actual condition. Would Freud agree that repressed wishes and feelings constitute "a state within the state, . . . a personality within the personality" (p. 315)? Is Miss E's split, as it were, horizontal, or vertical? Does she manifest a single personality caught in deep conflicts which impede her normal life, or does she exhibit two distinct personalities? If the latter, how deep does this vertical split go?

13. Jung summarizes the case according to general lines of Freud's early theory: "the split-off contents of the mind are destroyed by being released from repression" but adds the remark "through an effort of the will" (p. 317). This raises the technical issue whether or not this is "orthodox" Freudianism, and the more important issue of understanding Miss E's condition. Jung says the best energy cure is to expose to the light the images that consciousness finds intolerable (p. 316). But was this Miss E's difficulty? If her consciousness was in fact split between her proper self and her improper sexualized self, can we say (1) this was due to ordinary repression and (2) the sexualized self was *unconscious*?

14. It is not easy to assess the mental status of another human being; it is that much more difficult to assess the status of a patient described in a brief report written at the turn of the century. Yet Jung's patient has characteristics which set her apart from the usual hysteric. Indeed, she seems more like SW than she does Freud's famous patient, "Dora" (in his 1909, "Fragment"). If this is true, and if Jung consistently saw a different, often sicker, group of patients, how might that affect the development of his own psychological theories?

We can address this question by examining another of his case reports and, in a later chapter, by considering his own life as reported in his autobiographical account.

"Association, Dream, and Hysterical Symptom" (1906) CW 2

Technical Terms

Transistivism; will-fatigue; reproduction measurement.

1. Jung says this case is undoubtedly one of hysteria (p. 355). (Here again we must note that his patient would not be classified this way according to current psychiatric nosology.) After reading the initial report, can one assess Jung's own feelings about the young woman and the source of her illness? How does she explain her complaints, especially the heat in her head?

2. Jung treated her for three months in 1905, during which time he gave her the WAT six times. Assuming her suffering was due to purely psychological causes, does three months seem sufficient time to cure her (note she had been sick for seventeen years)? But is treatment and cure Jung's major motivation for seeing her and for reporting his findings?

3. To the usual WAT Jung added the memory task of asking his patient to recall her association to the stimulus word; the column marked "reproduction" lists her responses. About the first test Jung says her responses were similar to those of people subject to severe distraction. How does he use this bit of evidence to judge the severity of her "complex"?

4. She participated with even less interest in the second test; her failure rate was nearly 40%. How does Jung explain this remarkable inability? And how does her relative improvement in the third test give Jung reason to say she pulled herself together? Could one then use the WAT to measure the effect of psychotherapy and so gauge the effectiveness of one kind of treatment versus another?

5. Jung notes that the time-extensions of each test, the average reaction times, vary according to her overall mood. How do they also represent "will-fatigue" (p. 371)? Is this patient similar to Miss E? Does she also require a new invigoration of energy? Although reading her test results yields us little information, we might reflect on her constant complaint: something is wrong with her head, e.g., her headaches, the heat from which she has suffered so long. Why might one suspect that this kind of symptom typifies severe psychopathology, like schizophrenia, rather than a neurosis? (Where do most people locate their essential self?)

6. Does Jung's patient have any grounds for complaining to him when she exhibits what he calls her "transistivism" (p. 373)? How does she appear to understand Jung's probing questions to her, for example, about marriage and houses on pp. 376–78? "The patient always feels slighted . . . people also despised her for her illness, which they interpreted as laziness" (p. 378). Is the patient entirely incorrect? How does Jung explain the onset of his patient's disease?

7. Jung says response 69, on p. 380, contains a clear description of his patient's complex. What is that complex and does it follow that she is unable to articulate her fears about childbirth to either Jung or to herself? When she giggles at Jung's analysis of these associations, can we assume that either she recognizes what he says is true, or that the giggling itself is a sign of her unconscious recognition of their truth?

8. In summarizing the tests Jung says sometimes the complexes (or "complex-constellations") meet one another, and sometimes they

do not. What does this mean? If they do not meet one another, of how many divisions of consciousness are we speaking?

9. In the section on dreams, Jung charges ahead and interprets immediately her stereotypical dreams of fire and blood (p. 384). Why? Why not let her associate to them and so build up slowly to an intervention? Does Jung feel rebuffed by the laughter and embarrassment which greet his first foray into interpretation?

10. Why does Jung wait to give her the interpretation of the meaning of the cats in her first dream? And how does he recognize that the mouse dream is connected intimately to the cat dream? How is each term in a state of "reduced concentration" (p. 387)? Would this be so for all patients in all cultures at all times?

11. Readers who are familiar with Jung's later writings, in which he developed his own psychology distinct from Freud's, may find these interpretations surprisingly fixed upon sexual issues. Yet not all the patient's sexual thoughts are amenable to interpretation: ". . . the analysis comes up against strong barriers here which the patient cannot break down" (p. 389). Is this a sign that Jung is inadequately trained or a poor therapist? Is there something in his patient which is beyond her personal control?

12. This latter question is central to the development of Jung's mature thought. For example, who is the Black Man whom the patient sees in her dreams and in her visions? Her association is to a medieval tribunal that sat in secret. How does Jung understand this interesting fact in this text? Is the rigidity of his patient's response to these visions entirely a matter of her extreme defensiveness? That is, should we understand her inability to comprehend these stereo-typed visions as the result of repression alone? (We consider these questions at length below when we read his autobiographical account, MDR, and works from his middle period.)

13. Immediately following the dream of the Black Man on December 2, she dreams of "Lord Jesus" on December 3. (Looking ahead, again, we note that Jung himself had similar dreams when he was a young boy.) How does Jung understand the emergence of Jesus in his patient's unconscious thoughts? How does he link the figure of Jesus with the Black Man and both with himself, the patient's doctor? And how does his patient respond to his tactful interpretations (p. 393)?

14. Immediately following these interpretations his patient yearns for her mother. Why? Was it Jung's interpretation which cooled down his patient's sexuality, or his tone, or something else? Yet immediately following this dream is another which Jung says has transparent sexual themes woven around him and his patient's mother. Is there anything in Jung's responses which justifies the

patient's feeling that he will "shout at her" and punish her? (Is her dream of a penis-worm coming out of her mouth typical of young girls who are repressed sexually?)

15. Stones, apples, and nuts appear in profusion in the eighth and ninth dreams. Are they identical to one another? Do Jung's interpretations require us to assume his patient had actual incestuous relations with her brother? What is the secret which she hides from Jung and will not yield even to his implorings (p. 399)? Why does Jung hope for a decisive dream prior to her discharge?

16. In the third section of the paper, "The Hysterical Symptom," Jung says the goal of analysis is to get information on intimate matters. How are these attached to the unconscious complex and how do dreams, the WAT, and free-association all serve as detours around it? Why can one not ask the patient for the meaning of her St. Vitus's dance symptoms?

17. In the last few pages Jung summarizes the case and speculates as to the likely causes of his patient's illness. How many distinct causes does he enumerate? Is any more significant than another? For example, how should we weigh the fact that she avoided school by increasing her twitching alongside the likelihood that she suffered sexual traumata while a child? And how do these facts in turn fit into the crucial element of the onset of her menses in conjunction with her mother's illness? (Does it follow that all children with similar experiences should end up as Jung's patient did? If not what additional factors must we enumerate?)

18. Was the treatment a success? How should we gauge the fact that in her last week at the sanitarium the Black Man returned (p. 405)? Was Jung surprised that upon returning home his patient was no better? How did he account for the failure of his treatment? Did he advance her recovery? ". . . the automatism of the illness secures itself a free road to unimpeded development because each complex strives to live itself out unimpeded" (p. 406). What does this mean? (Would Freud have agreed?)

These latter questions assumed increasing importance for Jung when he struggled to remain faithful to his understanding of Freudianism and, at the same time, to let his own complexes live themselves out unimpeded. It was his fidelity to the latter tasks which set him off from Freud. At the same time, it was through this struggle that he created his own psychological system.

II

SYMBOLS OF TRANSFORMATION:
THE BREAK WITH FREUD

Symbols of Transformation (1911/12) CW 5

In moving from an examination of the WAT essays to this major text we have put to the side Jung's study on schizophrenia, *The Psychology of Dementia Praecox* (1907) published in CW 3. It was and is a significant work. In fact, it was the text which brought him to Freud's attention and which formed the strongest element in their initial relationship. Its major arguments are similar to those we have seen already in the two clinical essays discussed above. All three are essentially applications of Freudian theory to the study of borderline and schizophrenic patients. While Jung's conceptions do not mirror Freud exactly, at that time they remained within the general domain of classical analytic doctrine.

This is not true of *Symbols of Transformation*, an essay on the published fantasies of an anonymous American, Miss Miller. When Jung began writing it he saw himself a defender and proponent of Freud. When he finished he realized the book would cost him his standing in the psychoanalytic movement and his right to retain the mystical sonship Freud had offered him. Of his many books, *Symbols of Transformation* is perhaps his greatest, his most personal, and his most provocative. First-time readers of Jung may wish to read both the epilogue, pp. 441–44, and the Miller fantasies before they set sail on the seas of Jung's investigations.

Introductions and Forewords

As I noted in my introduction, Jung rewrote much of this work when he revised it in 1950. Since the CW text is the official version and the one most readily available, I refer to it consistently. At the same time I compare it against the original English translation of the 1912 text where it seems appropriate. Also, the CW version contains a translation of the Miller fantasies, the length and substance of which pale in comparison to Jung's comments upon them. (See the appendix, "The Miller Fantasies," in CW 5, pp. 447–62.) As we shall soon see, the German title, *Wandlungen und Symbole der Libido*, "Transformations and Symbols of

the Libido," emphasizes for good reason the priority of the transformation rather than interpretation of libidinal artifacts.

1. In the "Foreword to the Fourth Swiss Edition," pp. xxiii–xxvi,
   Jung describes an explosion of psychic contents which prompted
   him to write the text. Where else have we seen him describe such
   explosions? Although the foreword was written in 1950, long after
   he had formulated the principal features of his Analytical Psychology, is it unrelated to his analysis of Miss E? What is Freud's
   "reductive causalism" of which Jung complains so vehemently? Is
   this a philosophical or a scientific dispute? And is it related to
   Freud's personalism (p. xxiv)?

2. "So, in the most natural way, I took it upon myself to get to know
   'my' myth, and I regarded this as the task of tasks" (p. xxv). Why
   is this so important to Jung and, by extension, to his patients? Is
   Freud's method, at least to the degree Jung understood it in 1911,
   incompatible with this injunction? Did Jung's patients have personal myths the growth of which his "reductionistic" attitudes prevented? Why does he term his own myths a rhizome from which
   he sprang?

3. Indeed, Jung says there is something evil in considering neuroses
   and even the psychoses as merely medical illnesses. Why must
   psychology look to the human sciences for additional help in com-
   prehending the inner workings of human nature? Does Jung's use
   of religious and mythological texts require one to assume that he
   himself believed in God? Is his dispute with Freud over the truth
   of religion? If so, why does Jung then refer to numerous religions,
   many of which are not compatible theologically with each other?
   Can the outright empirical claims of contrary systems be true? If
   not, why does Jung grant to religious beliefs importance for his
   scientific enterprise?

4. The foreword to the second Swiss edition tells us the interesting
   fact that the woman whose fantasies Jung investigates in the text
   was a patient of a fatherly colleague and he never met her in
   person. Did Freud ever analyze patients whom he had not met in
   person? If Jung did not know Miss Miller, but read only the
   fifteen-page account Flournoy published in 1906, upon whose
   associations can he draw when he wishes to expand and interpret
   her fantasies? If he has only his own knowledge and fantasies and
   investigations available, what must he assume to be true of his
   and Miss Miller's individual psyches?

5. Given his claims in this foreword, especially those on p. xxix, what
   kinds of discoveries about the mental lives of psychotics, or
   dreamers, or primitive persons would count as evidence *against* his

claim that there is a "long buried primitive mind with its host of images, which are to be found in the mythologies of all ages and all peoples"? If Jung is correct, should all sympathetic investigators find in Miss Miller's fantasies identical mythical prototypes?

Book One

I. Introduction

Technical Terms

Transformation of libido.

6. Jung says Freud's interpretation of the meaning of the Oedipus legend is a simple remark. Is it? Note the length and grammatical structure of Jung's opening line: why would he make it so grand? Is Jung's a simple remark as well? He returns to the theme of simplicity when he contrasts the "confusing impression of the infinite variability of the individual psyche" with the simplicity of the Oedipal legend (pp. 3–4).

7. Does Jung reject out of hand Freud's attempts to explain historical artifacts and historical personages? Why are these attempts necessarily incomplete? How does Freud's insight help us understand the Greeks as never before and show us that Oedipus is still alive? And if this is true, does it follow that we can gain new insights about individuals if we, as psychologists, investigate the "historical materials"?

8. If Jung is correct, does it follow that Freud discovered something about human nature which was not known, in some form or another, by the ancients? And if he did not, how can we explain the interesting historical fact that Freud and his many followers, including Jung, acted as if he did? If he did discover something new, that is, if his was a scientific achievement, what was that element? Was it unavailable before his time in any guise? Was it therefore *not* part of ancient psychology? And if it was not available to the ancients, how far can one extend Jung's claims about the ubiquity of certain psychological elements without contradicting Freud's discoveries?

II. Two Kinds of Thinking

9. This brief chapter distinguishes between two types of thinking: thinking with words and thinking with images or symbols. Of the two which is the more ancient? And which is the more powerful and evocative? Yet which is the more logically astute? "When an idea is so old and so generally believed, it must be true in some

way, . . . it is *psychologically true*" (p. 7). Why is this so? Are dreams also psychologically true? If so why are disputes about their meanings so heated and often intractable?

10. This raises the interesting question, why are dreams symbolic? In the 1911 text Jung answered immediately: in order that their meaning remain hidden (p. 12). Why does he drop this answer and proceed to summarize the opinions of Anatole France, Wundt, Jodl, and Baldwin? How does he use the latter to argue that thinking in images is older and, in many ways, antithetical to "directed thinking" in words? And how does this fact permit us to explain why the Greeks failed to create a technological civilization?

11. "One could almost say that if all the world's traditions were cut off at a single blow, the whole of mythology and the whole history of religion would start all over again with the next generation" (p. 25). Why? Must all persons at all times bend to this claim? If not, are those who resist the pull toward fantasy of a higher nature?

12. "What, with us, crops up only in dreams and fantasies was once either a conscious custom or a general belief" (p. 27). Does this mean that modern peoples have inherited from their ancestors these tendencies toward mythological thinking? What gives these archaic fantasies their objective, factual status? Is Jung saying we have inherited particular memory traces of our ancient relatives?

13. If this is not his argument, how can we understand his claims that there are in all personalities portions which are extremely archaic and around which the modern mind is formed? Why are the unconscious bases of dreams and fantasies only apparently infantile reminiscences (p. 28)? If they are not memories, how can we explain their ubiquity and their repetitiousness?

14. But is it correct to say that, since human beings belong to one species and share a single ancestry as well as mental structure, their myths and deep unconscious (archaic) heritages will be identical to one another? How is it that every German carries with him or her a bit of Faust (p. 32) as every classical Greek carried a bit of Oedipus? Is there any level at which one can say that Faust and Oedipus are themselves aspects of a single shared character? Who or what?

III. The Miller Fantasies: Anamnesis

15. Miss Miller describes her deep sympathy for Cyrano de Bergerac about whom Jung knows a great deal and forthwith links the play to Miss Miller. She had additional fantasies; does Jung believe she was very likely a reincarnated Egyptian priestess or that she

wielded a magical power over certain artists? (If he does not, would he believe the reports of contemporary mystics who claim to levitate above the floor, see into the future, or read one's mind by peering into a crystal ball?)

16. It would appear Miss Miller thinks highly of her capacities which she feels link her to great figures and thinkers of the past. Do they in fact link her to them in the way she imagines? If not, does Jung denigrate her claims? Does he feel she is successful in ordinary relationships with ordinary people in her life?

IV. The Hymn of Creation

17. Jung pursues this theme when he considers her compositions, especially her sea chanty, and her other poems, one of which she confesses was of a serious nature. Of her "subliminal" poem about creation he says it must be linked to her previous evening's thoughts and unconscious fantasies about the handsome sailor. And in turn he links it to her father imago (p. 44 and note 4). Why is the latter a better term than "complex," a term we first saw used in the WAT? But has Jung repudiated the basic methods of the WAT? For example, how does he justify interpreting her poems as one of deep sexual concerns?

18. How does our knowledge of SW's state help us understand Miss Miller's fantasies? Does he refuse to accept her likely claim that her feelings about poetry and creation are genuine? How does mythology offer consolation to the young girl who cannot bear her father's child? Does Jung think his analysis exhausts the meaning for value of the fantasies? (Note his remarks on p. 51, note 18; how might subliminal perception point to a *future* state of affairs? Is this mysticism?)

19. Hence the night-singer becomes symbolized in the representations and guises of the Creator, God of Sound, of Light and Love. (Jung added the disclaimer about the idea of God when he revised the text; why might he have done this?) This leads him to consider Miss Miller's reference to Job and in turn to consider Job's individual psychology: What is that thing Job feared most deeply? "The God-concept is not only an image, but an elemental force" (p. 57). Where does this force reside? Is Jung then claiming that God exists precisely in the way traditional theists claim?

20. The question of repression returns when Jung contrasts it with the transformation of libido (pp. 58–59). In these few pages he distinguishes himself from Freud on the grounds that the latter understands all instances of religious language to be products of

repression while Jung says they may as well be moments of *transformation of libido* (pp. 58–59). How are these two processes alike and how do they differ?

21. "The God-image thrown up by a spontaneous act of creation is a living figure, a being that exists in its own right and therefore confronts its ostensible creator autonomously" (p.60). Does this mean there is an actual, living God, who corresponds to the god-image, as we correspond to our reflection? Does Jung argue that his reading of Miss Miller's fantasies and his consideration of the New Testament texts permit him to prove God's existence?

22. Immediately following these pages we meet for the first time the term "archetype" (on pp. 64ff). Where else have we seen Jung speak of portions of the mind which acted autonomously and, at times, seemed to confront the conscious portion of the personality? In other words, how should we understand the relationship between his original concepts of "constellation," "complex," (and Freud's notion of the unconscious mind) and his new term, "archetype"?

23. Jung's understanding of mass psychology and the ebb and flow of spiritual customs is illustrated vividly in his comments on the abyss that opened up in European civilization in the two wars of this century (p. 71). To which portion of the mass psyche is he referring when he says it got the upper hand?

24. Does he find Miss Miller's concocted verses of any value whatsoever? Why are they harbingers of our general spiritual malaise? And, how is it that truly religious persons are fascinated with sin and sensuality at the same time they seek to distinguish themselves from mere natural pleasures?

25. Modern peoples consider religious dogmas to be among the most boring and driest possible subjects. In this they are deeply wrong, according to Jung's reconstruction of the development of Western spirituality. What happened between the Middle Ages and the age of Descartes such that the vitality of religious beliefs drained away? (Why must Jungian therapists be students of history and religion?)

V. The Song of the Moth

26. To this second poem Jung brings a long excursus into another section of Goethe's *Faustus*, and then back to his previous reflections on the origins of the Christian period. With what authority or on what grounds does he carry out these intellectual journeys? From there he takes us back, via Miss Miller's associations, to a play, and his to another passage in *Faustus*, to the bronzed helmsman.

Is this not an insult to true believers everywhere? Would most middle-class Westerners accept his interpretation of I John 4:12, "If we love one another, God abides in us" (p. 86)?

27. From these thoughts he moves toward a consideration of Egyptian religion, Christian mystics, ancient and modern poetry, and comments on medieval alchemy, followed by a long section on Nietzsche's poetry (pp. 86–99). Assuming most of us will not duplicate Jung's erudition on these matters, and granting him the accuracy of rendition and assignment, we can ask: Why pursue this curious path? Why pursue these themes across so many divergent roads and in such strikingly dissimilar texts and authors?

28. This question takes on added force when we read that one of his sickest patients reported a fantasy of the sun having a penis out of which the wind arose. Jung has no embarrassment in relating this obscene idea to one of the great and noble themes of Christian religion: the immaculate conception of Christ by the Holy Spirit in the Blessed Virgin. Assuming this man did not read the obscure text to which Jung refers, how must we understand his reproducing it—and reproducing it within an *asylum*?

29. Jung returns to Miss Miller on p. 109. He had not yet considered the moth imagery in her title, the sun and god ideas receiving the bulk of his efforts. From her comments on Byron, Jung reconstructs the reason she "chanced" upon the fragment from his poem and, via an association to another portion of Cyrano de Bergerac, he describes her conflict. What is that conflict and why does he say we cannot judge whether or not her yearnings are for good or ill?

30. "She thus allows us to peer into the dark abyss of her longing for the sun-hero" (p. 110). From what portion of her personality does this longing derive? Does the objectivity and intensity of her longing signify that there is a sun-hero somewhere, beyond the stars, waiting for her? If not, how can we explain the peculiar force which her own poetry exerts upon Jung, and other readers?

31. Who is the young dying god that sinks and rises, and why is it in winter that he descends toward death?

Book Two

I. Introduction

32. Numerous mystics, poets, and religious authorities, as well as primitive philosophers, have asserted that in the depths of the human psyche dwells a "sun-god" image or that the sun is a god, indeed, the chief god. Does Jung feel they are correct? How are libido, the sun, and the chief god all aspects of a single great *objective* fact?

33. Faust employs magic spells, signs, and alchemy to force the dark powers to do his bidding; is he a madman to whom none of us is related? His "key" is similar to the phallus; to what great objective fact is the phallus similar, indeed a symbol of? Why do pixies and goblins (and other magical helpers) wear funny little hats? Are they merely expressions of phallic libido (cf. pp. 127, 131)?

II. The Concept of Libido

34. According to Jung, why was Freud incorrect when he attempted to explain paranoia, in the Schreber case, as the result of the regression of sexualized libido? Why does Jung feel that his term "psychic energy" better describes the features of schizophrenia which he observed in his patients? How is Freud's conception of libido an *interpretation* of something about which we must remain ignorant?

35. Often schizophrenic patients spontaneously report ideas and fantasies which are identical to archaic religious beliefs or to ancient folk superstitions. How does Jung understand these events? And how does the schizophrenic's capacity to find similarities between sexuality and eating or the sun and moon illustrate one of "the most important discoveries ever made by primitive man" (p. 141)?

III. The Transformation of Libido

36. "With the growth of the individual and the development of his organs the libido creates for itself new avenues of activity" (p. 143). Why does Jung use this peculiar expression? That is, why does he emphasize the libido's "intentionality"? How does the libido "migrate" to overt sexual organs and so instigate overt sexual activities, like masturbation?

37. Suddenly we find ourselves reading about ancient Greek plays, sexual customs, Hindu mythology, and German folk expressions for penis. Why? If Jung is correct, ought we to find that the "phallic plow" is alive and well in our culture? If so, what institutions or objects in contemporary American life manifest its characteristics? (Cf. the shape of sports cars and audio equipment with figure 15, p. 151.)

38. One often finds that primitive groups use dancing and other rhythmic modes as major elements in their religious celebrations. Children and severely disturbed patients do as well. Why are these not merely regressions to sexual forms? Why does Jung admire the American Indians who required their braves to stand around a beautiful naked girl without suffering an erection?

39. Returning to the question of the archetypes and their permanence, Jung says instinct cannot be overcome or controlled *except*

through the intervention of a spiritual force (p. 157). If this is so, how likely a success is therapy that aims at controlling instinctual impairment through rational means alone? If Jung is correct, why must effective psychotherapy replicate in its essential forms the great and central teachings of the medieval church or any such body? Did Freud's theories and methods permit such replications? (Did Freud believe his work could replace the teachings and methods of the church or any religion?)

40. Jung ends his exposition with another flurry of mythological references, case reports, and observations on infantile behaviors. Few people can match his erudition: does that mean one cannot verify or challenge his claims except by duplicating his massive reading and clinical training? Why might young mothers and other persons who know children be capable of responding to his claims? Lacking these avenues are there no other ways for normal people to examine Jung's theory? Are his materials and stories beyond our wildest dreams?

IV. The Origin of the Hero

Technical Terms

Hypagogic; hypnopompic; ambitendency; regression of the libido; extraversion; introversion; shadow; collective unconscious; Hero; Terrible Mother; symbol (vs. sign).

41. This chapter is much more technical than its predecessors; hence the large number of technical terms listed above. Jung's style is also much altered. In fact many of his paragraphs sound like Miss Miller's own prose. Why might this be so? How are the previous chapters preparation for this account of the Hero? How does Jung justify his forty pages of exposition, again brimming over with arcane references and illustrations, when its object is a mere paragraph from Miss Miller's report? (Must we assume she was as well educated and erudite as her expositor?)

42. Miss Miller evidently had great difficulty with actual relationships; was this because she feared sexuality in itself or was there something "beyond" eroticism which accounted for her inhibition? Is this a moral failing on her part? While she imagines herself to be highly individual, her thoughts, according to Jung, are almost stereotypical. What accounts for this latter fact?

43. Although she was not a Catholic, Miss Miller might have benefited from a confrontation with authentic Christianity (pp. 176–78) represented by traditional Catholic dogma. Why would "rationalistic" Protestantism fail to give her adequate nourishment? How would

traditional Catholic dogma provide her an extraverted route toward regaining her "psychic well-being" (p. 178)? (Would merely mouthing traditional formulae suffice?)

44. Jung says his patients often dream of "theriomorphic" entities, when Miss Miller envisions for a moment the head of a sphinx. What elements of our common heritage do such symbols represent? Why does "repressing the instincts" always produce dreams or visions whose contents are stereotypical, indeed predictable? Given the latter, what can the analytic therapist conclude about patients whose fantasies match those of Miss Miller? How *far* back in time do such symbols reach? (And why are they symbols and not merely signs?)

45. How does Jung use the vision of the Aztec figure to verify his claim that "the danger for a woman comes not from the mother but from the father" (p. 182)? Why are the Indian and Black (Negro) "appropriate" representations of the "Shadow"? (This technical term replaces "repressed sexual personality" in the 1924 translation of the original 1912 German text.)

46. In a typical moment Jung passes from considering the Aztec's headgear, to a passage from Solomon, to two seventeenth-century hymns, to the fantasies of a psychotic patient who hallucinated his mother's hand (p. 185). How does he tie together these apparently diverse elements? And how does Miss Miller's nationality figure into her choice of the sphinx symbol? (Does Jung's description of America remain accurate?)

47. This leads to the theme of anality and anal eroticism. Why does Jung say his schizophrenic patient (p. 191) was in effect exhibiting an outburst of positive feelings when she smeared herself with excrement and asked how he liked her then? Must we accept his conjecture about the importance of following spoors of hunted animals if we are to grant him his claim about the importance of excrement in our common human cultures?

48. Jung is not easy to follow in these chapters, partly because he skips so quickly from one esoteric realm to another, leaving us breathless. But another reason is that he makes such rapid interpretations that most of us must pause. For example, fig. 18 shows a priest dressed up with a large fish draped over his head and over his back. How does Jung help us understand what would otherwise appear completely ridiculous? (Are there parts of our culture which must strike outsiders as equally silly? What types of persons would be aware of such features of their *own* cultures?)

49. ". . . sexuality as well as the sun can be used to symbolize the libido" (p. 203). Why would a Freudian, of 1912 at least, find this sentence unintelligible? But with what evidence and on what

grounds does Jung propose it? Another way of asking this is: what did Jung's sickest patients teach him about the origins of culture which no science could convey?

50. Freud had already written of the ubiquity of incest fantasies and the defense against them in 1900. Why does Jung find Freud's sexual theory inadequate to account for what is clearly a sexual conflict? The hero, to return to Miss Miller's fantasies, is always seeking something; some believe it is for direct sexual conquest of the original mother and the elimination of the father. Jung says there is another, deeper, level to this unquenchable desire. What is that deeper level? Would psychic health emerge if it were fulfilled completely?

V. Symbols of the Mother and of Rebirth

Technical Terms

Teleological explanations; self-regulating equilibrium; the devouring mother,

51. In this long tour de force Jung blazes along a variety of trails, most of which are only tangential to the Miller fantasies. Nevertheless, the argument remains coherent since all his illustrations and discussions focus on a single great issue: why the impulse to incest is both universally despised and yet universally acclaimed as uncanny, and in archaic cultures, as profoundly spiritual. From Miss Miller's single comment on a dream city Jung launches into an account of symbols of the mother, particularly the evil mother who devours her children. How does he link the two themes to Miss Miller?

52. The incest taboo is universal; does that mean all people everywhere desire sexual intercourse with their aged mothers? Assuming some people achieved this goal, would Jung allow us to say that they had, however distastefully, achieved their actual goal? Yet, according to his extensive research, numerous religious myths and religious artifacts seem to glorify what every culture officially condemns—and generally punishes with speedy execution. How are incest and other sexualized longings for the mother a "symbol" for what is otherwise completely unknowable (p. 222)? How can the symbol of Christ (or any authentic symbol) *transform* us (p. 232)?

53. Some Christian theologians said that the Holy Ghost impregnated Mary, apparently through the ear. Why does Jung allow us to conclude that this—absurd as it might be as a scientific account of procreation—is "spiritually true"? Indeed, why does it make Jesus

that much more believable as both a solar hero and as the central object and ideal figure of Christian life? Indeed, why is it the duty of the scientific psychotherapist to respect at least the possibility of the *transformation* of libido through the intervention of Christ? (Is this an indirect apology for Christianity alone?)

54. "There must be contained in this feeling many dim memories of the animal age, when there was as yet no 'thou shalt' and 'thou shalt not'. . ." (p. 235). How does this claim permit Jung to explain why phantasms, myths, nightmares, hallucinations of psychotics, sublime portraits of Mary and Jesus, Hindu mythology, most of Egyptian mythology, and numerous other artifacts represent the mother as both immensely desirable and, at the same time, immensely dangerous?

55. Immediately following a description of pagan beliefs about sacred snakes and beetles (p. 269), Jung discusses the cross upon which Jesus died and likens it to a sacred marriage and Jesus' death to a moment of orgasmic union. Is this not sacrilegious? On what authority can he link the greatest tragedy of the Christian era to a common, if not sordid, portrait of gross sexual union?

56. We return to Miss Miller and, once again, Jung invokes the name of Faust who wishes to follow the sun and drink its "streams of quenchless light" (p. 272). How is this beautiful wish, in turn, tied to Miss Miller's view of a cliff, and her mysterious finale, "wa-ma", wa-ma"? When people are in great pain or great danger, as on battlefields, do they speak like Miss Miller, too? If so, can we assess her psychic state at the conclusion of this portion of her visions?

VI. The Battle for Deliverance from the Mother

Technical Terms

Individuation; the self (or Self).

57. Miss Miller envisions her hero riding a horse. From this fact Jung moves to consider the devil's cloven hoof, a fantasy of a neurotic patient, and a dozen or so other mythological sources dealing with horses. How do we know that horses may signify the passage of time, and that this seemingly abstract idea is but another representation of Libido, the *tertium comparationis*? Why do devils ride on three-legged horses (pp. 280–81)?

58. Returning to Miss Miller, we learn her hero, Chiwantopel, bravely bares his chest to his enemies' arrows. How does Jung connect this isolated theme with scenes from Shakespeare's *Julius Caesar*? What common element, shared by Jung, Miss Miller, and the

author of *Hamlet*, provides us the justification to make such outlandish comparisons?

59. Miss Miller is a young woman; her hero is a young man. Why does this not argue against Jung's claim that the hero represents an aspect of Miss Miller's own psyche? If we say the masculine hero represents a masculine part of Miss Miller's psyche, are we thereby ruling out the possibility that men might also create fantasies of a masculine hero? Can men be wounded by their own arrows as well? And if so, why does it follow that such suffering may not be merely neurotic? How does the presence of archetypal fantasies signify the sufferings of an age or a whole nation rather than an individual? (Cf. Jung's many comments on Nietzsche and Wagner.)

60. ". . . the constellated archetype is always the primordial image of the need of the moment" (p. 293–94). Given this claim, how would Jung understand or explain the rise and authority given to Freud's discoveries in the late nineteenth century? Why should we, therefore, pay special attention to Freud's religious background? And, in the same way, how would Jung understand the rise of his own archetypal psychology at this time and in this way? If the collective unconscious is the home of all potential symbols of transformation, why does not every age or eon exemplify each symbol equally? (Are there introverted ages of history just as there are introverted ages of individuals?)

61. The title of this long chapter announces another heroic theme: the hero must struggle back to the mother and, at the same time, struggle against complete regression. Why? What unthinkable danger does the mother represent? Why does the fear of living an actual life encourage one to turn "inward"? Is this Miss Miller's fate? And why should romantic poets, like John Keats, find themselves compelled to write about dangerous and fateful mothers to whom they are drawn yet who are, at the same time, dreadful and devouring (p. 298)?

62. The mother archetype appears in numerous guises, which seems understandable since each culture has distinct customs and representations of maternity, yet it also evokes completely contradictory feelings: those of immense and deep attraction, and the contrary ones of fear and horror. Does this or any other archetype exert "feelings" toward the ego? If not, how can we account for the tremendous feelings they evoke in those who approach them?

63. For example, how might one symbolize the phrase, "entry into the mother" (p. 301)? Of the numerous jokes, myths, and renditions available to one, which appear to be the most powerful? That is, which evoke the most laughter or horror or disgust? How

did Nietzsche's apparently original poetry and philosophy in fact re-express what was once common knowledge? Given Jung's explication of the dangers facing the hero, and given Nietzsche's place in bourgeoise German academia, what, most likely, was his fate? (As we shall see, Jung felt very close to Nietzsche and Goethe: what helped him avoid the former's grim end?)

64. In the same way, Miss Miller's fantasies resemble the great myths and stories of past civilizations and past religions. But do they protect her in the same way as the authentic myths protected their believers? "Chiwantopel is a typical animus-figure" (p. 304): why is his dream fate a direct sign of Miss Miller's own struggle? Is Jung optimistic or pessimistic about the outcome of that struggle? Is there any way one might have helped her do battle with her demons?

VII. The Dual Mother

Technical Terms

Enantiodromia; union of opposites.

65. In this long and vivid chapter Jung sounds a theme about which he never ceased to think: the birth of consciousness as a phylogenetic and ontogenetic event. "She who understands" means the mother. Does this mean that Miss Miller's basic difficulty was over unconscious homosexual feelings which so disgusted her she fell into a severe neurotic condition? Her hero seeks understanding; how do the original meanings of terms like *comprendre* and *erfassen* illustrate the universality of Miss Miller's animus's longings? Miss Miller's fantasy is typical of numerous myths, but she is in danger, as her subsequent collapse verifies, while archaic peoples are *not*. What protects them but fails to protect her?

66. Miss Miller finds her fantasies marvelous poetic moments. Why is she wrong in this assessment? Many other poetic young men and women manifest similar feelings about their internal life—indeed, many people find Jung and his psychology equally fascinating and uncanny. Why are these feelings incomplete, if not misguided? Why would seekers after the unconscious have dreams that are banal and everyday (cf. pp. 310–11)?

67. When he turns to consider Miss Miller's reference to Longfellow's poem, *The Song of Hiawatha*, Jung says we need not suppose that Miss Miller's fantasies were merely disguised memories of the epic. What provides him the theoretical justification to make this claim? How is the "teleological significance of the hero"(p. 314) itself sufficient to draw together Miss Miller, Longfellow, and, among other things, Coptic myths about the Holy Virgin?

68. From there we pass to a consideration of the birth of the hero, including Buddha and Christ. Each of them has an extraordinary history. Why must their births be so fantastic? Indeed, why must heroes typically have two mothers? Who or what is the second mother, and why is she always represented with such peculiar and extraordinary characteristics? How does Jung interpret the New Testament verse, "After me cometh a man which is preferred before me: for he was before me" (John 1:30)?

69. In a few condensed lines Jung assimilates the hero to the unconscious child, and it to consciousness, which in turn is born from a mystical power (p. 323). How does the god-image renew itself in the process of the hero's quest after his origins? From which side of consciousness, as it were, is Jung speaking when he says the "virgin anima" is turned toward the "inner sun" (p. 323)? According to this view, why was Christ born necessarily of a virgin and, at the same time, is said to be a son god and a sun god?

70. Standing outside for a moment from Jung's text, how do most people understand the process by which they emerged from nothingness, prior to their conception, to the fully conscious being they are now? Is ordinary consciousness an entirely coherent state of mind? Is that state ever threatened by dissolution or attack from within? If consciousness developed over time, both within the species and within the individual, might it also retrogress to the pieces or parts of which it is composed? What feelings does such regression arouse?

71. Jung reports that a patient responded with much uneasiness when he explained to her the meaning of water symbolism (p. 326). Why is her spontaneous remark about the jellyfish a verification of Jung's explanation and an example of the ego's usual response to first touching archetypal elements? What additional associations to jellyfish might she have had?

72. People in overt psychotic states, many mystics, and most myths describe the phantasms which confront them as real, objective, things, like sea monsters or evil, external forces. Are these reports entirely false? Are they entirely true? Where ought we to locate the "anthropoid psyche" (p. 328)? Why are "Freudian theory" and religious authorities aghast at the yearning toward regression which psychotics manifest and upon which Miss Miller's fantasies touch?

73. It might appear that Jung has explicated fully the psychological dimension of the hero: he represents, by projection, the personality's attempt to return to the sacred and original mother—the mother and source of consciousness. Yet we read, "The hero symbolizes a man's *unconscious self*, and this manifests itself empirically as the sum total of all archetypes . . ." (p. 333). Does this

contradict Jung's initial statements? When would this latter statement be true? At which part of the hero myth would one find all
the archetypal figures merged into a single entity? Does the
Eucharist contain such moments?

74. The theme of eating and being eaten re-emerges when Hiawatha
fasts. How does fasting contribute to the task of "creating oneself"? Alongside the highminded and abstract teachings of ethical
tasks the Christian church promulgates doctrines which announce
that God suffered for our sins, died on the cross, and returns to
His true followers at the height of the Eucharistic meal when His
flesh is eaten and His blood is drunk. How does this theological
claim differ from the "god-eating" practiced by archaic Mexican
tribes (p. 339, note 58)?

75. We learn that there is a church in Bologna built upon the remains
of a temple to Isis. To enter it one must creep through a tiny door
(p. 346). Why would this church appeal to Jung, especially given
what he has said about the non-Christian deities, Isis and Osiris?
Initiates of all sorts, including young people joining college societies, are asked to bend low and typically walk under the legs of
senior members of the cult? Why? And how are those requirements in turn linked to Christ's three-day vigil in hell and Jonah's
residence in the "great fish"? (Must we assume that the official
rulers of college fraternities are expert in the history of religions?)

76. "The sun, rising triumphant, tears himself from the enveloping
womb of the sea and, leaving behind him the noonday zenith and
all its glorious works, sinks down again into the maternal depths,
into all-enfolding and all-regenerating night" (p. 355). Do we
believe the sun dies at the end of every day? If not, why are
Jung's few lines so powerful and moving? Can modern peoples
share any part of the wonderment which Jung (and most scholars)
attribute to archaic peoples? How do modern, sophisticated persons view their own eventual sinking into the west? At what point
in ordinary lives would we expect to find the question of the sun's
descent taking on special urgency? (How old was Jung when he
felt compelled to compose this book?)

77. Miss Miller's associations touch upon Wagner's hero, Siegfried,
whose life and deeds parallel those of so many other heroes, particularly his incestuous origins. Wagner composed his dramatic
pieces in the late nineteenth century, an age that saw itself on the
verge of creating a new, fully rational society. How does Jung
permit us to explain, therefore, the sudden appearance of both
Wagner and his one-time admirer, Nietzsche, and, a few years
following, the creation of Analytical Psychology itself?

78. There follows a detailed analysis of the Siegfried legend and

Wagner's rich and complex elaborations of it. Most ordinary people do not adore Wagner's operas; few in fact would care to follow Jung's exposition. Does that mean that the archetypal themes Jung finds in it are not available to ordinary persons? Lacking access to Wagner are most of us therefore cut off from authentic contact with unconscious representations? If Jung's general theory is correct, where in modern, popular culture must we find themes and stories *identical* to those which appear in Wagner and in classical mythology?

79. Uneducated Christians have believed always there are dark forces, evil powers, and anti-Christ figures who struggle for the possession of their souls and against whom they must struggle with the aid of Christ's direct spiritual intervention. Are they wrong? On the other side educated Christians, since Jung's time, have denigrated as mere superstitions the plethora of underground demons, witches, and other satanic figures with whom the peasant seemed overly concerned. Are the cultured wrong too? How is Christ, as fully God and fully human, precisely the hero who combines in himself these two dimensions of human experience? How is he the "ruler of the inner world" (p. 368)?

80. Myths, like psychotic fantasies, are extremely difficult to follow; they have no apparent logic, no obvious point, and are full of grotesque and even obscene actions. In fact, persons and gods typically turn into their opposites: a mother becomes a destroyer, death becomes rebirth, and Christ the giver of life becomes Christ the bringer of death (He comes with a sword). Why are these signs of the vitality and authenticity of mythic thought? Why do they manifest so often an "enantiodromia" (p. 375)?

81. After quoting one of Nietzsche's more gruesome stories, about the shepherd who found himself bitten in the mouth by a huge snake, Jung says this was a fatal case where compensation was impossible (p. 380). Did Nietzsche also believe the case was fatal? Since it was Nietzsche's dream-vision, what can we conclude about his own psychic condition? Was it also fatal? (Nietzsche was raised the son of a Lutheran pastor and grew up to become a brilliant classicist; are these elements of introversion or extraversion?)

82. Freud once stated that in the unconscious there is no death. Does Jung agree? What is the mortal part of human beings and what the immortal part? Primitives, we have learned, typically say the end of the day is a time when the "sun dies in the west." But no one has ever seen a day in which the sun failed to rise in the east. Hence, the myth cannot be historically or even plausibly true. What then is the deep anxiety which lies behind this universal mytheme? Why is the dying god so often a sun-god?

83. (Jung added the last section on Christ when he revised his original
    1912 text.) Its argument derives from his later period and uses
    terms, like "quaternity" and "four functions," which are new to us.
    We consider these themes at length in their more fully developed
    form. However, they let us raise a final question about the hero: of
    what great and unnameable fear is he the universal representation?

VIII. The Sacrifice

In this final chapter Jung summarizes many of the themes he developed in the previous chapters and gives us his assessment of Miss Miller's
total psychic state. On what grounds can he do the latter, since he in fact
never met the lady? Why can one not protest that surely her fantasies
are merely ideas she found attractive (or loathsome)? Her hero is killed,
bitten, and immolated; why is his fate and annihilation a sign of his
creator's actual disarray? And why is Miss Miller's fantasy too easily
overlooked as mere diversionary chatter by a nervous young lady?

84. On pp. 398–413 Jung quotes extensively from poems by the great
    romantic German poet, Hoelderlin. How does his life and work
    exemplify one of the two routes the libido may take in its inexora-
    ble search for transformation? Many of Hoelderlin's poems are
    evocations of an idealized state of union with a maternal nature.
    Not finding her, or finding she is still unwarmed by his yearning,
    produces depression. Depression is not a pleasant effect; most
    people who are near it strive actively to turn back, employing
    every manner of drug, sexual activity, and the like toward that
    aim. Why are they wrong? Why ought they to regress consciously
    back to their earliest memories and feelings (p. 404)?

85. Are their fears entirely unreasonable? What are the dangers of
    sinking back into childhood memories, and from those back into
    even more archaic feelings and fantasies, to the "potential" psyche
    (p. 408)? How might well-devised religious myths, myths which
    retained their potency, aid the person who, like Hoelderlin, find
    themselves pulled back into and down to the *prima materia*?
    (Why would they imagine external objects and fearsome creatures
    are "out there" trying to harm them?)

86. Miss Miller could not face the demands of regression alone: she
    killed the hero, many times over. Why was she correct? Yet, Jung
    says, what was demanded of her was not very different than what
    Christ demanded of his followers: to die in their old selves and be
    reborn through their sharing of his triumph. What prevented Miss
    Miller from joining herself to that ancient stream of archetypal
    insight?

87. The central theme of sacrifice emerges in Jung's condensed statement, "To the extent that the world and everything in it is a product of thought, the sacrifice of libido that strives back to the past necessarily results in the creation of the world" (p. 415). What does this mean? He refers to a Vedic hymn and then describes the original state of unconscious, undifferentiated being, a union of mother and child. In such a state where is individual consciousness as we know it? If individual consciousness requires differentiation from the mother (or mother-environment matrix), why is the yearning for reunion with her (or Her) so dangerous and therefore so frightening?

88. "The world comes into being when man discovers it. But he only discovers it when he sacrifices his containment in the primal mother, the original state of unconsciousness" (p. 417). Given this, how can we understand the frequent complaint of psychotics that their external world is fragmenting and dissolving? More so, given Jung's fundamental claim, why should we expect to find that myths like that of Tiamat and Marduk (p. 415) dominate the cosmogonies of archaic cultures?

89. "In reality the neurosis is manufactured anew every day" (p. 420). Why does Freud's general theory of the neuroses (according to Jung's rendition) in effect massage the neurotic's ego and so prevent deeper insight into his or her actual fears? How do incest fantasies (and their corresponding anxieties of the primal scene— viewing parental intercourse—and castration) amount to a fixation of the libido onto a purely sexual and individual plane?

90. In addition to the sacrifice of the libidinal aim of reunifying oneself with the eternal and original mother, there is another required: the sacrifice of the animal, in Miss Miller's fantasies, a horse. The first sacrifice amounted to the creation of the world (as a place differentiated from the self and independent of it). The second "signifies a renunciation of the world" (p. 421). What additional regressive stage does this second sacrifice allow us to reach? How is the animal sacrifice the offering up of one's animal nature?

91. Jung's exposition of the meaning of the animal sacrifice, which would seem to lie near the heart of the Christian faith, becomes particularly opaque on pp. 424–25. What characteristics of the libido, particularly when it operates in a highly regressed state, account for the fluidity with which distinct symbols take on opposing and sometimes contradictory characteristics? Does Christian myth have themes analogous to that of Pentheus and his mother (p. 425)?

92. "We have learned in the course of this investigation that the libido, which builds up religious structures, regresses in the last

analysis to the mother . . ." (p. 429). Why to her (or Her) and no further? Does this psychological theory permit us to escape the necessity of carrying out the ritual acts we now understand? Where does the actual transformation occur? Why are science and scientific pretensions, when taken to extreme, sure to elicit the most dreadful of impulses: the sacrifice of all to the terrible mother? How does the Christian sacrifice transcend those of archaic religions?

93. In the centuries following the age of reason and enlightenment Christian dogmas were rationalized and made coherent with the dominant physical and metaphysical beliefs of the time. How did these intellectual apologies deprive dogmas of their authentic power? Can we understand Miss Miller's "failure" in part as the result of the dessication of dogma through the triumph of rationalism? Why do Jung's patients—persons who are hospitalized with "mental disease"—report to him, again and again, fragments of ideas which were at one time regnant religious beliefs? Might authentic dogma have saved Miss Miller from her own fearful fate?

94. Mental illness is considered in our times to be the expression of either faulty neural functioning or the result of inadequate parenting (or both). Given the argument and passion of this essay on transformation, what else must psychiatrists and psychologists learn before they confront their sickest patients?

III
THE ADVENT OF ANALYTICAL PSYCHOLOGY:
BASIC THEOREMS

"The Theory of Psychoanalysis" (1913) CW 4

"Psychoanalysis and Neurosis" (1916) CW 4

"Correspondence between Dr. Jung and Dr. Loy" (1914) CW 4

"Prefaces to 'Collected Papers on Analytical Psychology'"
(1916) CW 4

"The Transcendent Function" (1916) CW 8

"Instinct and the Unconscious" (1919) CW 8

"The Role of the Unconscious" (1918) CW 10

"General Aspects of Dream Psychology" (1916) CW 8

"The Structure of the Unconscious" (1916) CW 7

As we learn from chapter six of *Memories, Dreams, Reflections*, immediately following the publication of *Symbols of Transformation*, Jung broke with Freud. He then plunged into a "confrontation with the unconscious," a period in which he experienced many psychotic-like episodes. But these were not barren years. The nine papers we consider in this chapter bridge the two great periods of Jung's middle life: they constitute his intellectual struggle to distinguish himself from Freud and to establish, scientifically, the basic theorems of his own system.

"The Theory of Psychoanalysis" (1913) CW 4

When compared to the fireworks and drama of *Symbols of Transformation*, this essay will appear almost prosaic. It is certainly academic and didactic: we miss the intense, even idiosyncratic, force which Jung expended upon his masterpiece. However, this 1913 essay states clearly what was often left unsaid in the book on Miss Miller. For those who know Freud's early theory Jung's essay will appear less significant than for those to whom the entire period is new. However, both groups will profit from the essay for it reveals how Jung understood Freud's basic theory and it conveys his fundamental critique of that theory. (Freud discusses this paper in his "On the History of the Psycho-Analytic Movement" [1914: SE 14].)

Technical Terms

Psychic energy; prospective function of dreams; undifferentiated and differentiated libido; adaptation; regressive activation; moral capacity; teleological significance; empathy; transference.

A Review of the Early Hypotheses

1. Is what Jung says of the trauma theory, pp. 89–90, generally true today? From which period of his work do the majority of people, including scholars, draw for samples of "Freudian" theory? What was the "unknown anatomical source" (p. 89), which traditional theories of hysteria held was the organ responsible for the generation of hysterical symptoms? (Consider the etymology of the term "hysteria," and cognates like hysterectomy.) Charcot, and later Freud, rejected this purely anatomical theory in favor of a theory which emphasized the "traumatic" origins of hysterical symptoms. Good enough: but why link, in turn, traumas with hypnotic states? What experiential elements do both states share? Are these elements similar to what we observed in Jung's subject, SW, when she entered into her somnambulistic states?

2. "Repression" designates a key concept with which Freud overcame a severe problem for the trauma theory: how did it help him explain why different children suffering identical traumas will manifest different responses? Some will develop full-fledged symptoms; others show no sign of disease or discomfort. How does the "automatic mechanism" of repression account for these observable differences? How is it an aetiological theory (p. 94)?

3. It appears Freud abandoned slowly a fully physicalist or organic theory of hysteria. How was the theory of sexual trauma a bridge conception between the standard biological theories of the nineteenth century and more purely *psychoanalytic* ones? Yet, following up the trauma theory, Freud found that many of his patients reported events which could not have occurred. Hence the apparent traumata were actually imagined; not suffered. On the other side, Jung reports that even patients who suffered actual traumata, like the young woman caught in the St. Petersburg massacre, exhibited later behaviors which were inexplicable. Why must we investigate the "daemonic and capricious" ways we acted in our childhoods? (What are "daemons"?)

4. And yet it is not simply childhood traumata we must investigate. There is something further, something so forbidden it could not

be investigated prior to Freud: infantile sexuality. Jung says Freud's essay on that topic, in *Three Essays on the Theory of Sexuality* (1905, SE 7), aroused indignation and outrage. Do such notions outrage the majority of people in our times? If not, what has happened in our century such that most people can see that most children engage in "polymorphous-perverse" sexuality?

The Theory of Infantile Sexuality

5. Here Jung announces his basic disagreement with Freud: the latter's concept of sexuality is too broad. Why does Jung wish to distinguish between a "nutritive instinct" and "sexuality" ? According to Jung's summary, Freud says the infant's sucking at the breast is an example of (oral) sexuality since it incorporates the general qualities of sensation of tension, object seeking, and release of need through a pleasurable activity. (What other features does nursing share with adult sexuality?) Why does Jung prefer the term "emotional mechanism" (p. 105)? ". . . one of the instinctual systems is not developed at all, or is quite rudimentary" (p. 107). On what grounds does Jung claim there are at least *two* such instinctual systems operating within the infant? How does this distinction differ from the one Jung ascribes to Freud when he says, "Then the act of sucking the breast would be a nutritive act and at the same time a sexual act, a sort of combination of the two instincts" (p. 107)?

6. After summarizing Freud's general conception of multiple strands of sexual instinct, Jung says it is comparable to the state of physics before Robert Mayer's work on the conservation of energy (p. 109). (Mayer's work was championed by Brucke, at whose Institute Freud studied in the late 1880's in Vienna when he trained in physiological neurology.) On what grounds does Jung see himself as doing for psychology what Mayer did for physics? Are the two sciences equal in the degree of their development or in the accuracy with which they can measure "energic events"?

7. ". . . perversions . . . exist at the expense of normal sexuality, and . . . increased application of one form of sexuality follows a decrease in the application of another form" (p. 109). Jung says this and then gives an example of a young man who alternated between homosexual and heterosexual activity: does this case illustrate Jung's claim? Does it also prove it? What kinds of counter examples would one have to adduce in order to argue against Jung's "single quotient theory"? Can one measure the quantity of neutral energy Jung seems to describe here? Would Jung's argument account for people who become hypersexual in both homosexual and heterosexual encounters?

8. Freud's "conception of components, of separate modes of functioning, began to be weakened, at first more in practice than in theory, and was eventually replaced by a conception of energy" (p. 110). Who felt it was weakened and who replaced it? Why does Jung say we should recall that Cicero and other ancient authorities used the term "libido" in ways far broader than that of Freud's? Would this criticism deflect Freud from his claims? That is, does Freud have a way of explaining why theorists, especially rationalists, prior to himself failed to understand the existence of "polymorphous sexuality" in children—and themselves?

9. Jung says the theory of libido he proposes deprives "the sexual components of their elementary significance as psychic 'faculties' and gives them merely phenomenological value" (p. 112). Where else have we seen Jung explain sexual themes and fantasies in terms of their "phenomenological values"? How does he use this notion to explain the young man's reversion to homosexual relationships? Do all young men, disappointed by a heterosexual affair, retreat to homosexual activities? All in all, would this young man be surprised or shocked or angered by Jung's interpretation of his sexual behavior?

10. The following sections are a little confusing: Jung appears to disagree with Freud about the sexual nature of libido in general (recall how he used the term in *Symbols of Transformation*) but accepts the idea that infants and children may manifest sexual characteristics. But not all orality is sexual: why not? Upon what basic principles does Jung distinguish the "three phases of life" (pp. 117ff.)? Why is Jung so fond of the caterpillar analogy when he describes these separate stages? (Are there similar analogies in the religious myths and fantasies he described in *Symbols*?)

11. What kinds of observations of young children, those less than five years old, would Jung require in order to retract his basic claim in this section? Are pre-five-year-olds interested in any aspects of their genitals, or those of their parents or siblings? Do they exhibit behaviors or fantasies or dreams which one could properly term sexual? Most people cannot answer this question immediately. What additional information or observations ought one to make before drawing a pro- or anti-Jungian stance? (Would the analysis of adult or adolescent children yield any valid information? Would cultural products, like religious beliefs, exhibit in their content or structures themes which derive from this earliest period?)

12. This essay debates Freud's fundamental theorems. We cannot read it adequately without knowing those theorems and understanding Freud's reasoning for them. However, we can ask a pertinent, though difficult, question: given Jung's criticism, and

assuming Freud recognized the problems associated with them, why would he stick to his sexual theory of the libido in the face of so many obvious points against it? Jung's adoption of a theory of psychic energy would seem to have the virtue of bringing psychological theory closer to the queen of the sciences, physics, and, at the same time, identifying psychic energy with a neutral conception of energy in general. In other words, if Jung's propositions are so persuasive and obvious, why would Freud resist them? What *scientific* reasons might the latter have had for refusing to align psychoanalysis with the abstract laws of physics?

13. "Libido is . . . the name for the energy which manifests itself in the life-process and is perceived subjectively as conation and desire" (p. 125). From what point of view does Jung make this claim? Why does he stress the primary undifferentiated libido that causes cell growth? How does he link the growth of cells to the "differentiated" states he describes on pp. 125–26? And how, in turn, are these linked to the descriptive versus the genetic point of view in psychoanalytic theory?

14. In his condensed understanding of infantile perversions Jung appears to follow Freud's basic theorems as he announced them in his *Three Essays on the Theory of Sexuality* (1905) [SE 7]. Without having that text to compare alongside Jung's we cannot disentangle easily which author is claiming which theorem. But Jung makes himself clear enough: why does he prefer to say that libido *gradually* frees itself from its original resting place?

15. In part 4, "Neurosis and Aetiological Factors in Childhood," Jung carries out this program. How does he use it to explain the infantile features of neurotic sexuality? At the same time how does he characterize their capacity to face stern reality (p. 130)? Are their failings avoidable in some way? Are these moral failings which better training or better parenting might have prevented? If therapists cannot rely upon their patients' reports about their traumatic past, what can they rely upon when they wish to explain the aetiology of their patients' current neuroticisms? (Who "lacks courage" to change his mind once certain insights have occurred?)

16. How are the father and mother imagoes potential sources of later neurotic conflicts? In which portions of the psyche does Jung locate the origins of neurotic fantasies? ". . . Patients continue to hang on to forms of libido activity which they should have abandoned long ago" (p. 133). What is the meaning of the term "should" in this sentence? Is the "parental complex" a necessary feature of all neurotic fantasy systems? Is it a necessary feature of *all* individual fantasy systems?

17. In section 5, "The Fantasies of the Unconscious," Jung summarizes

briefly typical objections to the psychoanalytic conception of the unconscious. Why ought the psychoanalyst to be especially interested in mythology and the history of religions? Why might Freud have chosen the term "Oedipus complex" when he named the core conflict of early childhood? (Is Freud primarily an empiricist? Did he begin with a unified theory and deduce likely consequences of those basic assumptions? Is Freud's "empiricism" partly responsible for his inductive approach to theory of instincts?)

18. Does Jung say Freud's basic method of dream interpretation is revolutionary and particularly difficult? Why are the historian of religion and the psychoanalyst alike in their methods and orientations? Again, lacking an acquaintance with Freud's text, *The Interpretation of Dreams* (1900) [SE 4 & 5], we cannot compare easily Jung's arguments to those Freud advanced. But we can ask: if Jung's description is accurate, why was Freud's theory held to be revolutionary? There are numerous philosophic and literary interpretative methods, including those of history of religion. Why did their adherents fail to produce the insights (or at least claims) one finds dominating Freud's text?

19. After touching upon the use of the Word Association Test Jung moves to a central disagreement with Freud: the status of the Oedipus complex as the core conflict of infantile and hence neurotic life. He also recalls the major claims he made in his *Symbols of Transformation*. Is the Oedipus complex "only a formula for childish desires in regard to the parents" (p. 153)? Why would this reformulation make the topic "more acceptable"?

20. According to Jung, Freudians say the central anxiety associated with the Oedipus complex is the fear of castration. First, what does this mean and what kinds of observations or associations would one require in order to verify it? Second, how could young girls fear castration? Third, surely most parents never threaten their children with bodily harm, much less cutting off a part of their bodies. From which sources, then, do children derive the idea that they are in danger of suffering what Oedipus suffered (symbolically)?

21. ". . . Religion is one of the greatest helps in the psychological process of adaptation" (p. 155). This is no small claim: it separates Jung from Freud and it distinguishes his system and values from those of his mentor. For example, what are the differences between Freud's penchant for terms like "castration anxiety" and "incest barrier" and Jung's choice of terms like "sacrifice" and "conservative adherence to earlier attitudes" (pp. 155–56)? Are there episodes in modern history to which Schopenhauer's ominous warnings bear resemblance?

22. According to Jung, why did Freud go wrong in tracing back to their infantile roots the meaning of his adult patients' conflicts? If childhood neuroses are not the cause of adult neuroticisms, how are the two kinds of disturbances related to one another? Which parts of his patient "stage managed" her dissociated state in the face of the runaway horses? How much responsibility for her adult difficulties should we attribute to her or to certain parts of her personality?

23. "The 'amnesia of childhood' is an inference from the psychology of the neurosis, just as is the 'polymorphous-perverse' disposition of the child" (p. 164). By what routes does Jung link this criticism of Freud to the young woman whose case he describes on these pages? Does Freud hold that infantile and adult (neurotic) forms of sexuality are identical to one another? (Relevant Freud texts are in addition to *Three Essays on the Theory of Sexuality*, and the theoretical sections of his case histories, "Fragment of an Analysis of a Case of Hysteria" [1905, SE 7], "Notes Upon a Case of Obsessional Neurosis" [1909, SE 10], "From the History of an Infantile Neurosis" [1918, SE 17].

24. It happens, Jung says, that Freud's followers misunderstand the importance of the aetiological significance of the actual present (pp. 166–68). How does Freud's concept of the regression of libido in fact argue against an exclusive concern with the history of neurotic actions? On the one hand, the Oedipus complex dominates the unconscious fantasies of neurotics; on the other hand, if it is a universal complex and the single source of adult neuroses, why are not all adults neurotic? What additional factors must we assume produce the outbreak of an actual neurosis?

25. Jung pursues this question in the next section where he employs the metaphor of the mountain climber (pp. 169–70). From what field of philosophy does he derive most of the terms he uses in this section? What is the force of his phrases, like "cheap pretence" and "cowardice"? Jung then contrasts two sisters, the elder of whom failed at a life task. Her sister was a "fine courageous girl, willing to submit to the natural demands of womanhood" (p. 173) and who suffered no neurosis. Her sister was neurotic; should we therefore conclude the older girl failed in some moral sense?

26. To what degree was the older girl responsible for her adult difficulties? She was "traumatized" by the sight of an exhibitionist; why was this *not* the source of her later difficulties? Perhaps she was overly sensitive and, compared to her young sister, overwhelmed by the difficulties of her adult tasks? Perhaps she was more vividly impressed or traumatized than her young sister? Does Jung allow her any of these ways out?

27. Another way out would be to claim that she had suffered even earlier traumata, situations about which she had no conscious memory yet which exerted their influence upon the whole of her subsequent development. Why does Jung reject this explanation as well? Is he correct to say, "Deeper impressions are to be expected only from experiences in late childhood" (p. 179)? How might one investigate the validity of this claim?

28. "Regression is thus in very truth the basic condition for the act of creation" (p. 180). How does Jung link this aphorism to the argument of *Symbols of Transformation*? Did Miss Miller get better by virtue of expressing her deep fantasies? How are neurotic fantasies in general of teleological significance? Does this mean one ought to pursue them to their "logical" or biological end? What disciplines would permit one to accomplish that end?

29. In part 8, "Therapeutic Principles of Psychoanalysis," Jung contrasts his views with those of Freud: How does the former's work with the Word Association Test allow him to say that neurosis only *appears* to have its roots in earliest infancy? Why is the "prospective" approach more scientific than the historical one?

30. Neurotics, like many primitive peoples, manifest extremely bizarre fantasies, typically of a sexual nature. Are these sick ideas not the obvious sources of their own illogical behaviors? How does the usual analytic relationship foster the patient's innate tendency to create fantasies, seemingly without end? How does brooding upon them, this time with the collaboration of the analyst, aid in resolving current conflicts and current difficulties? (Why does Jung argue in favor of a "future cause" as opposed, simply, to holding onto the trauma theory of the early psychoanalytic period?)

31. Jung claims many analysts of his time attempted to empty out the unconscious, to search out the historical source of each symptom, and to find the initial appearance of each fantasy. Why is this an impossible task? Why does Jung advance the metaphor of the diver who seeks buried treasures amidst the junk and detritus of unconscious fantasies? Assuming Jung's emphasis upon the prospective function of symptoms and fantasies is well placed, does he also reject entirely the search for historical antecedents to those behaviors? Is the latter a therapeutic endeavor?

32. With regard to the central issue of the transference, Jung says it is both the major element of therapeutic change and a major source of resistances to change and hence to regaining health. Why is the purely historical method of reconstructing the patient's past, even in the midst of strong transference feelings, unlikely to alter the patient's neurosis? Is it not scientifically interesting at least?

33. Must the transference be analyzed in all cases in order for people to gain relief from their neurotic (or actual) anxieties? Like many others, Jung notes that the office of the priest and the role of the analyst are remarkably similar. Were the cures of the Church, via confession, bogus and superficial? Yet, in our time, few people seem able to receive the benefits which confession offered to their predecesors: what has changed such that the priest can no longer rely upon immediate transference cures?

34. The patient obtains a number of advantages via the transference. Why are these typically sufficient to create the illusion of deep understanding and almost magical cure? Are there any actual benefits patients receive entering into the therapeutic relationship? Are the aims of analysis to make the patient into any particular kind of person, for example, a rational scientist or a good mother or a person with profound self-understanding?

35. Transference occurs automatically when the patient casts upon the analyst infantile expectations. What might some of these be? If the transference is resolved by dissecting those infantile elements and showing how they counter the task of adaptation, why can the analyst's own personality not remain hidden or, at least, unaffected by the patient? What is "autoerotic mystification" and why must the analyst forsake it (p. 199)?

36. In his discussion of dreams and their meaning, Jung would seem to leave himself open to the attack that, once more, he champions mystical nonsense when he says superstitious peoples have always understood the prospective function of dreams (pp. 200–201). Does this mean he believes dreams are accurate visions of future objective events? Which elements of the future are "predicted" by dreams in the present? (We pursue this question at length below in the section on dream theory.)

37. In the last section, "Future Uses of Psychoanalysis," Jung notes that medicine had not taken up Freud's science with completely open arms. Why is analysis larger than any single branch of medicine? Given Jung's claims about dementia praecox (schizophrenia) and our reading of *Symbols of Transformation*, what other sciences or humanistic disciplines might serve the goals of analysis equally well? Does Religious Studies have anything to add to this common task?

38. In section nine Jung summarizes ten interviews with an eleven-year-old girl whom his assistant treated. What weight and value does Jung attribute to the knowledge of fairy tales and myths for persons conducting analyses? (Would medical schools be a likely place to learn about such things?) Could treatment proceed without some awareness of the psychological meaning of such stories?

In general, how do most people treat such stories and little girls who apparently believe in them?

39. We learn that the girl has had intense sexual feelings about her male teacher and, indirectly, about her father. Why does Jung say we cannot conclude that it was these fantasies which caused her to manifest neurotic symptoms? What additional factors must we elucidate in order to explain why this particular girl fell ill with fantasies which are themselves universal? (Were there similar "environmental" issues in Miss Miller's life when she fell into her twilight states, described in *Symbols of Transformation*?)

40. Some other children had told the patient that a little girl had conceived a child by a boy of her age (p. 219). How does this bit of schoolyard "smut" figure into the patient's failure to consolidate the therapeutic gains won so arduously over the course of the treatment? What permitted the libido to escape along its old pathways? (Would this be true of rumors in general? Could rumors ever manifest an advanced form of psychological functioning?)

41. How would a knowledge of mythology and folklore enable the analyst to grasp more quickly the likely meaning of the little girl's fantastic hypotheses about the events which lead up to the birth of human beings? After referring us to numerous mythological parallels between the patient's fantasies and archaic beliefs, Jung returns to the issue of libido theory. But before leaving we ought to ask an obvious question: why is the same belief, for example that rain is seminal fluid, pathological in an individual yet healthy in a culture? We can assume that the patient's lack of "objective knowledge" permitted the efflorescence of fantasy, but it is the adults who maintain parallel beliefs in archaic cultures. Are not the latter capable of understanding the simple biological facts of conception and birth? If so, how can Jung account for the persistence of infantile beliefs among them?

42. Jung does not deny that the young girl manifested typical oedipal issues and fantasies. Why are these and the usual Freudian explanation of them, as he understands it, incomplete? Why does he prefer the notion of unutilized libido to the Freudian conception of repressed libido (p. 223)? In the same way would Freudians (or you) agree with Jung's claim that "she preferred to follow the secret promptings of puberty rather than her obligations to the school and her teacher" (p. 223)?

43. Analysis, Jung says, is a refined form of Socratic "maieutics" (p. 225). What does this mean? Would Freud have agreed with this claim entirely? Recall Jung's distinction between the young girl's regression to archaic fantasies and her "moral failing." Does he weigh each aspect of her character equally? Are there parallels

to each in Socrates' understanding of the ethical tasks of philosophy? (On the latter see, for example, the "Apology," "Lysis," "Gorgias," "Protagoras," "Meno," "Phaedrus," and "Symposium".)

44. Returning to the question of a "collective mind," a concept with which we shall become increasingly familiar, Jung notes that his discoveries of the parallels which exist between a child's fantasies and cultural myths suggest the old theory of a state of perfect knowledge before and after "individual existence" (p. 225). What does this mean? Are there similar concerns expressed in Plato's dialogues? If Jung, Plato, and the eleven-year-old girl have similar ideas about existence before and after life, how shall we account for this remarkable similarity?

We consider this question with increasing intensity as we proceed from considering these transitional works to a close examination of Jung's full-fledged analytical essays. Before doing that, however, we read three short pieces in which Jung distinguishes his method and orientation from those of Freud.

"Some Crucial Points in Psychoanalysis: A Correspondence
between Dr. Jung and Dr. Loy" (1914) CW 4
"Prefaces to 'Collected Papers on Analytical Psychology'"
1916/17) CW 4

Although these two short texts are not formal, theoretical treatises, they reveal many of Jung's major opinions on issues central to the distinction between his and Freud's theories.

Technical terms

Moral development; psychocatharsis; resistance; empathy; biological duties.

1. Jung appears pleased to respond to Dr. Loy's questions, at least in the beginning. How would you characterize the tone or style of the latter's correspondence, particularly the last few letters? Given what we know of Dr. Loy's position and hopes for his own treatment with Jung (pp. 252–53), what kinds of feelings and fantasies might we expect him to manifest to the senior man? (Does the junior physician verify or contradict the long citation he quotes from Freud regarding the need for a personal analysis?)

2. Dr. Loy says he has been disturbed by the severity which many neurotic patients exhibit when their "stored up" fantasies are stirred by hypnosis and other forms of intervention (pp. 254–55). Why is Jung not disturbed by the same kind of dramatic anxiety? Are the junior man's questions, in this letter, thematically consistent

with what we know of his original hopes for a relationship to Jung?
(Is it fair to ask these kinds of therapeutic questions about a
published correspondence?)

3. Jung once employed hypnosis; does he despise it now? Why did the
    discovery of Breuer's and Freud's book (*Studies on Hysteria* [1895],
    SE 2) seem to him a lifesaver? Is Loy correct when he says, p. 261,
    that Jung rejected hypnosis yet at the cost of rejecting the transfer-
    ence? About whom is Jung speaking when he writes, "the analyst is
    successful with his treatment just so far as he has succeeded in his
    own moral development" (p. 260)? How would the younger man
    have responded to this dictim? (On persons who failed to accom-
    plish this development see Jung's brief essay, "The Realities of Prac-
    tical Psychotherapy" [1937] in CW 16 (pp. 327–38).

4. Both men use the term "moral" a great many times. For example,
    Loy describes a moral conflict between love and duty (p. 263),
    while Jung had used the term, above, to describe the psychothera-
    pist's personality development. Are these identical uses of the
    term? Returning to the issue of transference, are the junior man's
    questions rare and especially perplexing? If not, why would he
    raise them here and with such intensity?

5. Jung responds with the statement that he is not a practicing physi-
    cian. Why would he say this at this point in their correspondence?
    He was seeing patients and carrying out a form of medical prac-
    tice (and he had earned an MD). Then why would he abjure a
    title which he had apparently earned? Does Jung feel Dr. Loy's
    description of the conflict between love of the truth and one's
    duty to one's patients is entirely accurate? How would the youn-
    ger man respond to Jung's remarks, "But we should ill prepare the
    ground for the seed of the future were we to forget the tasks of
    the present, and sought only to cultivate ideals" (p. 267)? Who
    should not forget about Kepler?

6. In the letter which appears to be the immediate response, Loy
    begins by invoking the New Testament, and then presents a leng-
    thy description of the metaphorical dimensions of truth, complete
    with a solar analogy. Does Jung, too, believe that clear definitions
    of fundamental ideas are necessary? What is the overall tone of
    Loy's letter, for example, in his comments about the errors of the
    Middle Ages and the tireless fight of defenders of the psychoana-
    lytic school?

7. What makes Jung respond to Dr. Loy with the remark, "You tell
    me what psychoanalysis is"? Was not the junior man originally an
    honest student of the subject matter in which Jung was an
    acknowledged master? Which kinds of patients are, according to
    Jung, among the most tiresome? Why would they be so? Jung says

he has but one working rule (p. 272). Why would this single rule prevent patients from developing magical expectations? (Is Jung's tone "fair"; ought therapists to remain emotionally neutral with their patients?)

8. In his letter of 16 February 1913 Dr. Loy points out a number of disagreements in the psychoanalytic literature, then raises the question of the patient's life after analysis (p. 274). Loy remarks that patients get well because they love the analyst; why does Jung reject this goal and explanation of treatment? Why is nothing finer "than the empathy of a neurotic" (p. 277)? Does this mean neurotics would make especially good therapists since they are so attuned to the intrapsychic life of others?

9. A popular picture of Jung is that of the mystic seer who plumbed the depths of transcendent knowledge and there discovered the fixed and unalterable meaning of sacred symbols. Does Jung himself agree with this general idea of the power and singularity of symbols? If not, is Loy correct when he worries about the purity of analytic interpretations. Might not clever and empathic patients read the analyst so carefully that they merely reproduce the analyst's own ideas and preconceived interpretations? If dream symbols are not fixed in their meaning, and if patients can mimic easily their analyst's style, what grounds the treatment relationship and keeps it on course? (Given this understanding, would Jung give much credence to the benefits of self-analysis?)

10. Again, Loy responds to Jung's sober statements with propositions whose tone is rather different; for example, the last sentence in his letter on p. 283. What is the younger man's general tone and with which sorts of persons and which sorts of circumstances does one come across similar exhortations? And given that, can we speculate as to the unconscious reasons which impelled him to address Jung in this way?

11. Jung has a great deal to say about the virtues and vices of the Catholic Church (pp. 283–85) and its sway over individuals. Indeed, he links the Church's ancient method of moral suasion with the Viennese school (Freud). How, according to this linkage, does Freud in fact advance the repressive traditions against which he originally struggled? Freud, Jung says, argued a *retrogressive* interpretation of transference: why is this only half the story? That is, why does a more complete interpretation of transference feelings include a notion of *teleological* direction?

12. Jung then advances a few comments on biological duties and the ways in which neurotics avoid them (pp. 286–87). Why would adolescents be especially liable to neuroticizing sexual drives, while more mature adults are more likely to discover the higher

good of the personality? What is the hierarchy of values to which Jung here pays obedience? Is a purely materialistic metaphysics capable of recognizing the teleological dimension of the values which make up this hierarchy? Yet are these higher values divorced entirely from any biological foundations? How are they like the birds' artful nests and the stags' antlers (p. 287)?

13. After remarking upon the ill effects of sexual hypocrisy, and noting the injustices which are visited upon women, both married and unmarried, Jung returns to the issue of religion, particularly Christianity. Why ought scientific psychologists to examine carefully its basic claims about the goals and fundamental yearnings of human beings?

"Prefaces to 'Collected Papers' on Analytical Psychology" (CW 4)

Technical terms

Semiotic interpretations; symbolic interpretations; prospective and retrospective values; finalistic point of view; regulative principles of thought.

1. These two short prefaces state clearly how Jung distinguished himself from Freud around 1916. They also employ technical terms which, we will find, take on increasing weight when Jung elaborated his fundamental conceptions of the archetypes and individuation. Does Jung view himself and his theories as absolute contraries to Freud and his basic claims? Why would Jungians feel their orientation is broader and more inclusive than that of Freudians?

2. According to Jung, the basic point of disagreement is the way in which Freudians interpret symbols. Why is a causal, sexual, and "semiotic" mode inadequate to the task of interpreting symbols exhaustively? What evidence do we have from our previous readings, especially Jung's thoughts on Miss Miller's fantasies, that neurotic and dream symbols may point the way forward, toward an end which is dimly perceived?

3. But surely Freud and Adler were intelligent men who recognized numerous examples of teleological behaviors? Given this, how does Jung explain their inability to grasp the synthetic truths which he and his followers have chanced upon? (How does William James provide him a useful way of describing both Freud and Adler?) What additional factors in the philosophy and method of both men account for their fondness for causal, natural, and reductionistic explanations of human psychology?

4. Indeed, is Jung saying that Adler and Freud have made what

amounts to false discoveries? If not, why can we not simply adopt their insights and go about our daily business knowing that we are, finally, the product of prior causes about whose aims and nature we must remain ignorant? Religion was the natural counterpart to such theories (does Freud disagree?), yet we cannot doubt many of its symbols are shopworn. How ought we to replace them? From what resources can modern peoples draw the new symbols which will carry out the functions and aims Jung assigns to those of Christianity? How can limited and completely modern, that is, agnostic, persons go about creating symbols that will help them overcome the very circumstances created by an environment hostile to symbolic truths?

5. Jung articulates two distinct reasons why Freud and other objective analysts are wrong about the meaning of aberrant mental processes. The first reason is related to the philosophy of science; the second is related to the general human need for symbols which will help one live (pp. 292–93). Does Jung claim that either of these reasons disproves or refutes Freud's scientific claims? What does he mean when he says religious symbols have provided effective devices of "moral education" (p. 293)?

6. Would Freud agree when Jung says that mere causal truths can do nothing but induce hopelessness and resignation? A question related to this is more difficult to answer but equally important: why do we still find passionate defenders of Freud who would dispute most of what Jung says about Freud, and passionate defenders of Jung who would respond with equal feeling and equal vigor to those who criticize Jung? Are there similar disputes in other sciences? Are there similar schools, for example, in biochemistry or geology or any of the natural sciences?

7. We return to this question in Jung's preface to the second edition of his papers where he tells us the first edition was met with contempt, especially in Germany. Readers of this work on Jung will have learned by now, if they had not seen elsewhere, that Jung's name evokes still in the majority of intellectuals distinct, often moralistic, opinions bordering on abuse. While with Freud he is dismissed by most academic psychologists, Jung is subject to a general condemnation and even sarcasm rarely visited upon Freud. Why might this be so? What elements of Jung's thought would set off such severe responses in persons who are otherwise willing to at least read an author before condemning his or her work? Does Jung himself anticipate these kinds of attacks?

8. Jung responds to a few critics and then, invoking the name and example of Kant, explicates the notion of "final cause" with reference to function, meaning, and aim (pp. 296–97). How, according

to this interpretation, does Freud err in searching for the meaning of a symptom in the patient's *past*? To ask this another way, where is the patient's past when he or she describes himself or herself in an analytic session? Why should we grant to the past an ontological status greater than that we grant to the future (for where is the future)?

9. Jung says certain critics surprise him by confusing his patients' beliefs with his theoretical formulations of the meaning of those beliefs. Ought he to be so surprised? Assuming these critics are not wholly malicious persons, what elements of Jung's style might foster these mistaken readings of his *scientific* beliefs? (Does one find that many of the people who identify themselves as Jungians also confuse Jung's beliefs with the rather more fantastic beliefs he ascribes to his patients or subjects?) This confusion becomes especially pronounced when one reads his paper on "The Transcendent Function" (1916). It is very easy to read this as a manifesto in favor of an anti-scientific point of view and as the utterings of a new, self-proclaimed prophet.

"The Transcendent Function" (1916) CW 8

Technical Terms

Transcendent function; active imagination; complementary attitude; permeable partition; symbolic vs. semiotic; constructive interpretation; self-regulating system; mythologems.

1. The preface to the essay is well worth reading, although Jung composed it some forty years after he had written the essay. On what grounds does he conclude that the fundamental and universal question asked by all religions and philosophies is precisely what he addresses in his essay? Is the unconscious a single portion of the psyche, or a part of the natural world, or determined by any single set of coordinates? If not, with what justification can we speak of it as a unitary phenomenon which appears to all peoples in all times the same?

2. Given this view of the unconscious (or the Unknown), why does Jung then advise us that while the method of active imagination is a royal road to uncovering its nature, it is fraught with diverse dangers? What kinds of dangers are these? (Do we find primitive philosophers and "medicine specialists" also speak of mysterious dangers which surround their work with spirits and the like?) Did Miss Miller, described in *Symbols of Transformation*, use active imagination when she elaborated her visions of the Indian romances?

3. Jung adds two characteristic comments: the task of integrating unconscious elements into one's conscious life is a *moral* one, and the West's undervaluation of the unconscious makes its appearances all that more dangerous. We will see him develop both opinions at length below; however, we can ask: what model of the mind underlies this rough quantitative claim? What kinds of things, mechanical or biological, become increasingly unstable or liable to destruction the more one aspect of their functioning is suppressed?

4. In the essay proper Jung outlines the major features of his model of mental functioning. From what domains does Jung draw the major theorems about the way the psyche behaves? Freud is accused often of engaging in wholesale reductionism and, worse, of championing a model of psychic functioning which is entirely mechanistic. Are there such mechanistic features in Jung's basic model? And if there are, so what? That is, why should one find the charge of either reductionism or "mechanization" one worthy of serious rebuttal?

5. In his very first paragraph Jung disavows any mystical intent by claiming that his concept of the transcendent function is similar to a concept with the same name in mathematics. To understand this central claim we have to know, first, what the mathematical concept is and, second, how Jung wishes to correlate it with his generalizations about psychic functioning. A quick glance back at the mathematical concept informs us that transcendent functions are those which cannot be expressed by a finite number of algebraic operations, just as transcendent numbers, like pi, are incapable of being represented by equations which have rational, integral coefficients. Hence one cannot say that pi = 22/7 or 3.141 . . . since it appears impossible to designate a final digit in the decimal representation. Given this, how strict is Jung's analogy between the two forms of transcendent functions?

6. For example, in the succeeding paragraphs, Jung outlines the major features of the conscious and unconscious systems; each system operates in a way which "compensates" the tendency and proclivities of the other. It might help to outline the four major differences Jung says characterize the two systems. On what grounds does he claim that an advanced civilization like ours requires a higher threshold of consciousness than that required by both primitive peoples and certain creative persons in our culture? Yet neurotics also have more permeable partitions separating the two systems; why are they sick while primitives and creative individuals with similar partitions are not?

7. The theme of rationality reappears when Jung attempts to elucidate how consciously directed problem solving operates. Why is

the fact that such judgments are based on what is known crucial to understanding how even the most open-minded rationalist thinks in a decidedly one-sided way?

8. More strikingly, Jung says in most cases the more strongly one holds a rational opinion, the more threatening becomes a counter-vailing tendency which is always unconscious (p. 71). Jung says this as a matter of course; would most psychologists agree with him? If not, what core features of Jung's model of psychic func-tioning does the latter not yet grasp? "But if the tension increases as a result of too great one-sidedness" (p. 71), disaster results. From which countervailing elements does such a tension arise?

9. Jung characterizes Freud's original therapeutic model as that of emptying out the unconscious, and so permitting the conscious mind to rule one's life unreservedly. (On Freud's conception of treatment at this time see his "Papers on Technique" [1911–1915] in SE 12, pp. 85–173.) Given Jung's model of the psychic appa-ratus, why must we conclude that one can never empty out the unconscious, and that treatment must be a readjustment of opposed forces, or tendencies? And assuming the latter is true, what kind of process must the therapist hope to see take place in patients nearing the end of their treatment?

10. Why can no "rational solution" perform the task of unification which Jung says marks the end of a successful treatment? (Is a rational solution analogous to designating a number as the product of rational coefficients?) If neurosis were caused by a severe trauma, suffered in one's childhood, could psychotherapy not aim at a once and for all cure? Why does Jung stress the importance of "attitude," while other theorists of his and our time stress the importance of prior causes, brain states, neurological functioning, family dynamics, and the like?

11. The therapist uses the transference to mediate a new attitude: how does the latter result from the unification of conscious and unconscious attitudes? Most transference issues appear to be child-ish or even infantile attitudes toward the therapist who is held responsible to effect a magical solution and so consolidate the patient's dependency. Freud argued against such solutions; is Jung arguing in their favor? If not, how does Jung account for the ubiquity of infantile sexual fantasies in neurotics, particularly in their conceptions of their therapist?

12. To illustrate his disagreement with Freud, Jung describes a patient's dream and then compares what he claims is a Freudian interpretation of it with his "constructive" interpretation (pp. 75–78). How is the first interpretation semiotic and reductionistic, while the second is symbolic and expansive or constructive? Of

the two, which would most patients prefer? (Again, not having access to Freud's work we cannot challenge or support Jung's claims directly. But does the term "phallic fantasy" (p. 76) entail necessarily the claim that the patient's thoughts are wholly regressive and infantile?)

13. Most patients would not have Jung's extensive knowledge of mythology and related subjects, like medieval alchemy and Gnostic religion, and so could not expand their associations easily. Why can the Jungian analyst feel free to aid them along these lines without incurring the charge of mere suggestion?

14. Jung reveals the extent of his disagreement with Freud and the radical difference between their theories when he goes on to review and assess the sources of unconscious materials. In addition to dreams, the therapist has available the behaviors Freud described in his earliest books: parapraxes (like slips of the tongue), intrusive fantasies, and, most importantly, symptoms. All of these are inadequate to the task of generating the transcendent function. Why? Why does Jung favor, instead, behaviors controlled by conscious choice, like directed fantasies, artistic renditions, and the like?

15. In the face of such an argument the Freudian of this period might well consider Jung simply indulging his and his patient's anxieties about facing their own infantile yearnings and so concocting elaborate defenses against insight. Assuming Jung's model of the mind is valid, why would the Freudian critic be wrong? Which elements of the psyche's self-regulative operations *guarantee* the validity of Jung's synthetic, constructive mode of therapy? In fact, does Jung believe all cultures suffer necessarily the conflicts and neuroses which dominate our lives in the West? If not, would they have any need for either Freudian or Jungian psychotherapists?

16. Jung's acquaintance reported a dream in which he stepped out into space from the top of a mountain (p. 81). He laughed at Jung's warnings. What gave Jung the capacity to predict this man's unhappy fate? Would the latter have been so disdainful of Jung's advice if he had lived in a culture which valued dreams and other messengers of the unconscious? In this regard, does Jung contradict Freud's emphasis upon techniques, like "free-association," which therapists use to deepen and expand a neurotic mood? Are the other methods, like art and automatic writing (recall the case of Miss SW), exactly like what Freud termed "free association"? If so, why do most Freudians *not* employ them, while most Jungians do?

17. This raises again the task of distinguishing both the models of psychic functioning each man employs and the way each values

the cultivation of the unconscious. Would Freud grant to the
workings of the unconscious as much autonomy and directedness
as Jung does? This also causes one to examine the distinct way
each man understands the meaning of symptoms. Jung includes
them among the minor signs of an imbalance between conscious
and unconscious systems; is this compatible with Freud's basic
formulations? (See, for example, Freud's essays of the same period, especially "The Unconscious," and "Instincts and Their Vicissitudes" in SE 14).

18. Having raised up unconscious materials to consciousness, one must
now respond to them: what appears to determine one's choice of
the two methods Jung describes? Could one learn to acquire an
intuitive, aesthetic approach to the unconscious? In other words,
could patients acquire a new talent through the benefits of psychotherapy? (Do people enter psychotherapy with these kinds of
goals in mind?)

19. Jung returns to his fundamental theorem when he says there is a
danger in overvaluing either of these tendencies (p. 84). What
behavioral signs indicate the presence of such overvaluations?
Sometimes one feeling predominates, at other times its exact
opposite: on what grounds can we predict that these kinds of
feelings will *always* form pairs in which one member is the opposite of the other? Although one cannot create such tendencies,
Jung says therapy aims at bringing forth both: why? If a patient
happens to be gifted artistically and learns to employ that gift,
what general tendency *must* we find dominates his or her *unconscious* orientation?

20. According to the concept of ego put forth here, can it by itself
initiate the processes which will culminate in the appearance of
the transcendent function? If not, and if the transcendent function is precisely that which indicates the possibility of psychic
health, how can an individual guarantee his or her mental health?
For example, would a thorough understanding of Jung's psychology provide one an innoculation against being surprised by one's
unconscious orientations and wishes?

21. "It is exactly as if a dialogue were taking place..." (p. 89). Where
have we seen Jung carry out this precept? (Again, it would be a fascinating and worthwhile task to compare this ideal to Freud's fundamental conception of treatment.) Is the concept of an internal
dialogue alien to either classical Greek ideals of self-knowledge, or
to Christian ideals of self-restraint? More surprisingly, Jung argues
that failure to recognize this other self distorts necessarily one's ability to perceive "outer objectivity." Why?

22. Jung then advances a claim which will reappear throughout his

later writings and to which we shall pay a great deal of attention: the balancing of two polar attitudes constitutes a new level of functioning, not a "logical stillbirth" (p. 90). First, what does he mean by the term logical stillbirth? A brief return to Aristotle's logic or to any textbook on logic will prove helpful. According to these general, logical analyses, how must one treat a proposition which includes opposing claims, that is, contradictory statements?

23. Is Jung arguing against the validity of these general logical rules, like the law of non-contradiction, and in effect saying anything goes? If he is, how can he protect himself from the criticism that given a set of contradictory assumptions one can prove anything, and therefore any nonsense may be advanced with no possible check? If he is not claiming this, where does he locate, as it were, logical rules and other restrictions to which most scientists and philosophers pay obedience?

24. It is difficult to find two pages which state more succinctly Jung's fundamental point of view, and illustrate why he is counted among the irrationalists by persons in the natural sciences and others, like Freud, who adopt the sciences as models for all forms of inquiry. For example, why is the prejudice against mythologems as silly, according to Jung, as a prejudice against the veracity of the duck-billed platypus? Why would Jung find this odd creature especially appropriate for his argument? Have we seen already similar oddities in the fantasies and other products of persons who are engaged in the struggle to bring forth the transcendent function?

25. Jung concludes this admittedly sketchy essay with a few remarks on the goals of treatment and what it requires of a patient (pp. 90–91). Does one find these requirements typify medical treatment in our time? Do most physicians require their patients to manifest courage and other moral virtues in order for the treatment to work? Does Jung expect a great new medical breakthrough, somewhere in the future, will enable us to forego the tedium and anxiety associated with the practice of psychotherapy in our time?

"Instinct and the Unconscious" (1919) CW 8

Technical Terms

Instincts; unconsciousness; learning; intuition; personal unconscious; collective unconscious; archetypes

1. Although brief, this essay forms a crucial link between the Freudian and neo-Freudian essays we have considered so far and the explicitly Jungian works we will examine below. In it Jung

employs the term "archetype" for the first time and, more importantly, gives us a detailed exposition of the way he intends to use
the term. To do that he refers to Rivers' definition of instinct: why
can the psychologists not adopt this directly and wholeheartedly?
Is Jung's objection a moralistic or theological one?

2. Persons who know Freud may find Jung's discussion particularly
difficult to follow since, unlike Freud, he argues that phobic
responses are not direct expressions of an instinctual apparatus
(p. 131). Why does the fact that they occur sporadically argue
against their instinctual basis? Are not such phobias products of
unconscious processes which are, in turn, grounded upon some
form of instinctual occurrences? If neurotic phobias were ubiquitous, and not idiosyncratic, would Freud be justified in explaining
them as the products of instinctual conflicts?

3. On what grounds can we say that intuition is the "reverse of
instinct" (p. 132)? What is the relationship of this mode of knowing to the general portrait of the psyche Jung advances in this
essay? According to his definition, can one say that persons may
intuit the content of their "personal unconscious" ?

4. In rather condensed lines Jung goes on to distinguish a variety of
unconscious processes and types of unconscious organizations (or
levels). Which characterizes the kinds of thoughts and feelings
Freud identified as "the unconscious" and which sought he to
uncover via psychoanalysis? Over and above, but also below, these
are what Jung terms the collective unconscious. (Before investiga-
ting that concept, can one identify Jung's evaluation of Freud's
theory? Is he contradicting what he represents as Freud's basic
understanding, or is he "expanding" the older man's theory?)

5. The collective, one might say, has two kinds of content: one the
archetypes, the other the instincts themselves. Why is this, finally,
inadequate to the task of clarifying the relationship between these
two phenomena? Jung says it is hard to answer these kinds of
questions; some experts say one thing, others say the opposite.
Given his own explication of the concepts collective unconscious
and archetypes, is there any direct way one might catalogue the
contents of the collective? If yes, how would one know there was
no more to discover? If the correct answer is no, what attitude
must one bear therefore to any claims of completeness—in either
depth psychology or religious studies?

6. If Jung is correct about the nature of the instincts and their relationship to archetypal images, why *must* Freud be wrong when
he, supposedly, attempted to delimit the boundaries of the unconscious and to "empty out" its contents via psychoanalytic treatment? In fact, if Jung is correct, why are Freud's method and

theory dangerous and destructive? And if they are the latter, what kind of attitudes toward all other sciences must such practitioners manifest if they are to avoid the dangers Jung says lurk near them?

7. Jung is not hesitant to link his concept to that of philosophers and theologians of ancient times. Is this amiable attitude toward pre-modern thought typical of scientists or of most contemporary psychologists? Would they too chart the historical ups and downs of a concept which they purport to explicate as the latest and most comprehensive truth of their disciplines?

8. Among the most revolutionary of contemporary theories in the social sciences is that of sociobiology. Its adherents argue that complex social behaviors are determined by the subtle interplay of "hard wired," genetic structures. Is Jung's use of the yucca moth in this 1916 essay pertinent to these general sociobiological arguments? Do yucca moths need to explain their remarkable treatment of the yucca flower? Does their lack of an explanation retard their ability to carry out this ancient ritual? Humans also act in complex ways; must we assume that their self-conscious explanations of those actions are necessarily correct?

9. The concept archetype is typically subsumed under the notion of internal images upon which the conscious self stumbles as it regresses from active, rational processing to prelogical forms of thought. Is this the notion we find in this essay? Why does Jung say the archetype *determines* the mode of apprehension? (How does the yucca moth know which of the numerous flowers in its environment is the single one without which it and its offspring will perish?)

10. Jung says Rivers' criterion of the all or none reaction allows him to designate the appearance of instinctual processes: how? And given this, why is he keen to correlate the concept archetype with precisely this version of instinct theory? For the first time we glimpse his marriage of instinct theory with his fundamental valuation of religion: "In the great religions of the world we see the perfection of those images" (p. 137). If this is so, and keeping in mind his reference to the yucca moth, why *must* any authentically scientific psychology come eventually to a point of affirming the *biological* value of religion? More so, why must we conclude that so-called primitive religions will tend to be more authentic with regard to their representation of archetypal forms than are highly rationalized faiths?

11. But few modern thinkers recognize these facts (just as few contemporary readers of Jung would include him among the sociobiologists). Most modern persons have no inkling of mythological

concerns or mythological modes of perception. Why are they, and even great thinkers like Freud, wrong? Indeed, if Jung is correct, why is it more accurate to say that severely disturbed people like Miss Miller (and Jung himself during a difficult period in his life) perceive better the depths of our common human nature?

Jung says rightly of this essay that it sketches out ideas which he was to fill in with more subtlety and depth in the works of his later period. But before turning to those, it will pay us to consider a popular lecture he wrote two years after this piece. In "The Role of the Unconscious" Jung expands upon his conception of the archetype and reveals its implications for a general social psychology.

"The Role of the Unconscious" (1918) CW 10

Technical Terms

Personal unconscious; archetype; collective unconscious; symbolic function; repression vs. suppression; Jewish mentality; projection.

1. Ever since the middle-1930's, when German and most other European scientific societies were Nazified, Jung has been accused of various degrees of complicity in the persecution of Jewish scientists and intellectuals. Complicating this issue is the undeniable fact that Jung's essay for the newly Nazified *Zentralblatt für Psychotherapie* was perfectly congenial to Nazi racism (see CW 10, pp. 157–173). (He says very little about this issue in MDR; I list pertinent sources in the appendix to this book.) Given that this essay was published more than a decade before Hitler and the Nazis came to power, can one claim that Jung was influenced by the ideas of the Fuhrer? If not, how ought one to account for the similarities which obtain between certain themes in Nazi race "science" and certain themes in Jung's social psychology?

2. After summarizing some of the philosophic doctrines which preceded the appearance of dynamic psychiatry, Jung says the concept of an unconscious mind became important only when clinicians used it to investigate psychopathology. Jung then says he himself investigated the concept fifteen years previously, around 1902–1903 "independently of the Freudian school" (p. 4). Is this entirely correct? He appears to be referring to his medical dissertation (1902) and to his studies on word association, both of which we have read. To what degree does Jung rely upon Freud and Breuer in both these texts? (Recall our discussion of this point. Could Jung have formulated his concepts of splitting, symptomatic expression, and "subpersonalities" without the benefit of Breuer's and Freud's formulations on hysteria?)

3. In his summary of Freud's basic theory Jung strikes a new tone: what is the rhetorical effect of terms like "lumberoom," "smuggled," and "reductionism"? An assessment of Jung's portrait of Freud becomes especially difficult as we read texts from this and the later periods since it is rarely clear as to how well each man continued to read and understand the works of the other. For example, by 1918 Freud had recast much of his theory of "the instincts" and, by definition, altered substantially his views on sexuality as a central, intrapsychic phenomenon. (See his 1914 essay, "On Narcissism: An Introduction" [SE 14], which is explicitly a series of tentative formulations.) Yet, according to this article, why is libido theory hopelessly out of date?

4. Experiences and memories no longer available to one's conscious are still available to "the unconscious." How does the example of the effects of reading suggest a rationale for Jung's explication of subliminal perception? Although he does not say so, might one use this to explicate the concept of collective subliminal perceptions as well? That is, might the particular form archetypes assume in particular cultures be products of similar experiences which leave behind similar long-lasting traces?

5. Given Jung's description of the personal unconscious and the deeper structure upon which it rests, why does it follow that (1) the human brain determines the shape of archetypal fantasies, and (2) all human beings will share, at a fundamental level, the same set of mythologems? Are the latter just another form of the doctrine of inherited ideas? (Is Jung Lamarkian in his theory of evolution?)

6. Jung's comments upon the value of modern science, as well as modernity in general, strike many people as nothing other than sheer romanticism or, worse, antirationalism in the guise of a pseudo-science and pseudo-religion. Are these evaluations of Jung's philosophy of science accurate with regard to Jung's *intentions*? How does Jung account for the rise of modern science? Why is it in fact anti-scientific to suppose that modern peoples can or have overcome the need to take seriously the collective unconscious? (Would collective elements enter into rational, scientific formulations? For example?)

7. How does Jung move from these considerations to his analysis of racial psychologies (pp. 12–16)? Who else had written of the "blond beast" (p. 13), the lower half of the German psyche, "ready at any moment to burst out with devastating consequences"? Why does Jung stress the role of Christianity in creating this split in the German mind? Are there other European nations whose conversion to Christianity paralleled that of Germany? If so, ought Jung's warnings to hold for them as well?

8. With hindsight, and enlightened by our knowledge of Nazi Germany, Jung's language may appear, at best, ill-informed, at worst as racist and psychotic as the speeches Joseph Goebbels wrote for Hitler. To tease out the scientific rationale for these claims from mere speculations and, perhaps, popularized racialist propaganda is no small task. But it is an important one. For example, with what logic does Jung connect his speculation that Jews live "without feeling the power of the chthonic" (p. 13) to his conclusion, "these [Freud's and Adler's] specifically Jewish doctrines are thoroughly unsatisfying to the German mentality; *we* still have a genuine barbarian in us who is not to be trifled with" (p. 14, italics mine)? Is Jung proud of this blond beast?

9. "I like to visualize the unconscious as a world seen in a mirror" (p. 17). Why does Jung like this metaphor? Why is he so keen on establishing the equality of the unconscious with the conscious? Indeed, what danger lurks for all of us if we refuse to see this essential truth? Recall Jung's brief recapitulation of the history of the West: at which point in time did the great revival of spirituality take place which led to the formation of contemporary Europe? Why is he especially interested in linking the rediscovery of the collective unconscious with the French Revolution? Returning to the mirror metaphor, are primitives wrong when they see the external world as ordered and maintained by "spiritual agencies" (p. 18)?

10. Jumping to another topic Jung deepens the notion of symbol considerably when he compares the "symbol-creating function" (p. 18) with the compensatory function of the unconscious. Why is the first only relatively existent, while the latter is necessarily present any time conscious and unconscious processes co-exist? Although the compensatory function operates automatically, it is not necessarily strong enough to balance off a one-sided orientation. If so, what *must* one do from the side of consciousness, as it were, in order to strengthen the psyche's ability to achieve a proper balance? How did Kant's rabbinical student fail in this attitude, and how did Jung's elderly patient succeed so that the "symbolic quality" of her dreams revealed itself?

11. As he did most notably in *Symbols of Transformation*, Jung explicates the meaning of the elderly patient's dream by reference to distinct issues in the history of religions, specifically, the conflict between the early Christian church and Mithraism. (For additional comments on Mithraism see the index to CW 5.) How should we understand the dream's representation of the bull with a broken leg? Is Jung at all correct when he predicts the logical outcome of a culture's denial of its animal nature? Was Germany

in the early twentieth century a Christian nation? (Was Hitler aware of the animal nature of the "German psyche"?)

12. Jung returns to the question of Freud's causal theory. Assuming he correctly portrays Freud's general line of argument, why does Jung find the sexual explanation inadequate to this patient's problems? Is it necessarily true that elderly people have no sexual concerns and no sexual conflicts? Is Jung denying this?

13. "Thus, when anyone in his conscious life is wholly under the sway of instinct, his unconscious will place just as one-sided an emphasis on the value of ideas" (p. 24). Recalling our discussion of the transcendent function, what general model of the psyche must Jung have in mind when he makes this global claim about psychic functioning? If he is correct, would we expect effective psychotherapists to adhere to any single set of therapeutic principles or techniques? If the answer to this is no, then what will characterize the truly effective psychotherapist?

14. Jung describes two forms of projection: one is negative; the other is positive. Can one always know what and upon whom one is projecting something that is actually true of oneself? In a later essay Jung will distinguish projections that arise from the personal unconscious from those that arise from the collective. From which psychic realm do those he describes on pp. 26–27 arise? Why is their magical quality a sure sign of their origin?

15. A bit of nature that is denied and even reviled always seeks "revenge." Can one understand, in part, the Nazis' portrait of the Jews as a product of the return of a split-off portion of the German psyche? Were the Jews considered or felt to be magical or uncanny or dangerous in some mysterious way? By whom? Given Jung's understanding of Western history, would he support those who explain German war crimes as the product of a single maniacal personality?

16. "We must begin by breaking it in ourselves" (p. 27). How can *modern* persons accomplish this goal, particularly if they have no way to engage in meaningful religious activities? Although Jung says cultural renewal must begin with individuals, are there collective products or institutions to which individuals can appeal for aid and direction? How can one guarantee the emergence of a "natural morality"?

(For further consideration of Jung's attitudes and explanations of the German state and the Nazis, as well as the aftermath of the Second World War, see his five pieces in part three of CW 10, especially "Wotan" and "After the Catastrophe." For comments upon his relationship to Nazi science and policies, see texts listed in the appendix.)

"General Aspects of Dream Psychology" (1916) CW 8

Technical Terms

Compensation (compensating factors); final causes vs. efficient causes; teleology; unconscious functions; mythical modes of thought; unconscious complement; projection and counter-projection; prospective function; imago; interpretation at the subjective or objective level.

This is not the first paper Jung wrote on dreams; it is the first to use explicitly his major theorems. Prior to it he had written "The Analysis of Dreams" (1909) and "On the Significance of Number Dreams" (1910/11), both of which explicated Freud's basic dream theory because "there is nothing fundamentally new to be offered in this field since the research of Freud, Adler, and Stekel. We must content ourselves with corroborating their experience by citing parallel cases" (1910/11, CW 4, p. 48). He did not continue to hold this opinion.

1. As we have seen previously, much of Jung's discussion is a dialogue with Freud. It is especially true of his remarks upon dream interpretation, which will make the most sense if one can compare them against Freud's fundamental theorems in his *The Interpretation of Dreams* (1900, SE 4 & 5). Given this, we can ask if Freud would agree with Jung's assertions about the "forward" and "backward" meaning of dreams: how are the first elements pertinent to the dreams' "hidden moral meaning" (p. 239)?

2. Jung summarizes a patient's dream about eating apples and suggests it illustrates the young man's moral dilemma. Is this just another version of a conservative and repressive moralism that attacks, as it were from without, the young man's deep and most personal wishes? If not, why does Jung call this aspect of the dream its moral function? How is the latter always in a compensatory relation to one's conscious attitudes? And why should the dreams' *moral* intentionality emerge in sleep, precisely when Freud had said that the rational functions lost their dominance?

3. Jung also disagrees with Freud's concept of the symbol: how does the final point of view permit us to examine not only the somatic referent but also the infinitely large number of meanings to which the unique dream element may refer? Assuming Jung is correct, can we use his method to explicate the range of meanings implied by his symbolic use of the concept "compensation"? What extended metaphors emerge from this primary notion? For example, he says the dream was calculated to open the young man's eyes: who did the calculation? Who or what led Miss Miller to create her fantasies about the Indian hero?

4. If Jung is correct about compensation and its ubiquitous appearance in all peoples at all times, ought we to find a similar belief in native or primitive theories of dream? Should not primitive philosophers and wise persons have intuited what Jung had to rediscover? How are dreams understood in fairy tales and other children's literature? Consider an example or two of dreams in this kind of literature: does it too manifest a "moral" concern analogous to that which we found in the "Apple" dream?

5. To consolidate our understanding of the final point of view it will be helpful to consider three or four "Freudian" symbols, like the famous cigar, from the point of view Jung espouses. (Consider also key and lock, house and balcony, tunnel and train, or other such sets of traditional symbols.) Would Jung or Freud claim he could interpret fully a dream symbol without the patient's corroboration or associations? Why is training in the history of religions an especially valuable attribute of the seasoned dream interpreter?

6. The original paper ended at this point the CW editors tell us. Jung added the remaining sections in 1948, a period well beyond the middle years about which we are concerned. However, the later section summarizes well much of his later thought and so provides a bridge for us to that period.

7. To illustrate his claims Jung describes a man's dream which apparently contradicted his conscious reasons for visiting him. How does the dream rectify the patient's conscious attitude? If this is a general truth, how must we explain other products of the unconscious which force themselves upon us? Would this be true of group projections as well? And if true of groups, would it also be true of entire nations and entire epochs of human history? (We consider this last question at length when we read "Aion" below.)

8. One might suppose that the theorem of compensation, like that of the transcendent function, if valid, would permit one to predict the exact meaning of manifest dream content, since the unconscious must be reacting to a definite, conscious constellation. Hence, if we can identify the conscious attitude, we should be able to predict its corresponding negation from the point of view of the unconscious. Why is this overly simplified? Why does the *consensus gentium* argue against this overly mechanical view of the unconscious.

9. Jung wishes to distinguish sharply the compensatory function of dreams from their potential *prospective function* (pp. 255–256). What features of unconscious thought processes permit some dreams to reveal a prospective, revelatory function? Yet dreams are not psychopomps. Who would assert otherwise? Given Jung's description of both functions, at what point in psychotherapy or

in one's life ought we to expect to find dreams that manifest both compensatory and prospective qualities?

10. Is it possible to idealize dreams and to expect them to solve impossible problems for oneself or one's patients? If so, how does the compensatory function, once more, come to the psyche's aid? What kinds of dreams will appear to people who strive to appear better than they actually are, or who wish to identify themselves with their idealization of Jung, or similar figures? Why would a thorough, "Freudian," analysis benefit such persons—indeed, all persons who wish to analyze dreams? Does Jung believe he has found a *single*, completely reliable method of dream interpretation?

11. After discussing five or six types of dreams, including those which appear to be psychic, Jung returns to the task of distinguishing his point of view from Freud's. What is the difference? Does Jung deny that some dreams are precisely what Freud said they were, disguised fulfillments of sexual wishes that are abhorrent to the conscious psyche? Why does he say a purely sexual reading of dreams reduces dreams to mere concrete problems?

12. Among educated peoples Jung is often thought of as a mystic or a petulant follower of Freud, who, out of jealousy and oedipal rage, rejected the older man's truths and spent a lifetime reacting against them and their creator. Does this judgment capture the tone of this essay? If Jung's concept of projection and its "normal" role in ordinary psychology is correct (pp. 264–265), how might he explain the bitterness and diatribes his name occasions? What attitudes and feelings characterize a full-blown episode of projection?

13. Using his own dream as an example, Jung distinguishes sharply between interpretation at the subjective level and interpretation at the objective level (pp. 266–270). Why is Freud's method essentially one of finding subjective meanings? Does Jung feel Freud is completely wrong? Naive persons believe representations of other persons are obviously "objective" since they are not identical to the dreamer's ego. Why are they wrong, yet why are Freudians wrong as well?

14. Jung argues a subtle point: an unimportant dream figure may disguise a much more important person about whom I dare not feel certain things; hence, I repress those feelings and use the dream work to carry out a safer mode of representation (namely, through displacement). How is the lawyer figure in his dream, on p. 268, better understood not as an "objective" referent to his patient, but as part of himself? Upon what affective signs can we rely in order to make this kind of judgment? And why is the presence of monotony an excellent sign that analyst and patient are pursuing incorrectly an objective line of investigation?

15. Jung turns to the broader question of social psychology, particularly with regard to the "legion" of projections which one notices in war time. In a sometimes sermonizing way he appears to champion the neurotic's willingness to face his or her own moral complicity. At what point in treatment does the neurotic come to understand the actual objectivity of his or her neurosis? What must treatment effect before the patient can gain this form of legitimate objectivity?

16. Analytic experience ideally promotes the capacity to undo one's projections, and so regain the energy which one expended upon their creation and constant refueling. Are there phylogenetic counterparts to analytic treatment? Religious systems, as we have seen, employ directly symbols and artifacts that pertain to projections (from the collective). Does this mean that religions consolidate projections and so hinder one's attempts to free oneself from the binds of the collective?

17. Although his last remarks are less coherent than the initial ones, since they seem to concern issues, like philosophy, which appear unrelated to the interpretation of dreams, Jung feels all psychic products are of a single piece. Why? Why are most physicans unable to perceive this simple fact? In the same way, why is Jung so confident that he, and we, can understand any religious system, no matter how contrary to our own and how irrational in appearance?

18. Jung concludes his essay with a reflection on God and the God-image. Why does he feel no conflict in affirming both that all peoples at all times have understood the nature of the god-image, and that science, including analytical psychology, can have no final say about the ultimate referent, God alone? (We see him address these issues directly in the six texts we consider in the next chapter.) However, before doing that we read one final essay, composed in 1916, which outlines his fundamental claims.

"The Structure of the Unconscious" (1916) CW 7

This brief essay marks a turning point in Jung's thought. It is of profound significance since he dissociates himself from Freud, and outlines the basic conceptions of collective unconscious and fundamental archetypes like the persona and the anima and animus. He revised it a number of times. In its final, much expanded, version it became the second essay of his text, *Two Essays on Analytical Psychology* (1928 and 1938), which comprises CW 7. (A major portion of the CW text is excerpted in Campbell, *Portable Jung.*)

Technical Terms

Personal unconscious; collective unconscious; libido; psychic energy; assimilation of the unconscious; persona; anima; animus; primordial images

1. Jung repeats many of his criticisms of Freud, particularly of the latter's supposed reliance upon the concept of sexuality to explain all of psychic life. Assuming Freud does claim this, why is the usual understanding of repression inadequate to the task of describing completely the nature of the unconscious as it is revealed in analytic experience? Why is the fact that patients continue to produce unconscious fantasies *after* analysis a telling criticism of Freud's portrait of the unconscious itself?

2. It appears that Schopenhauer and a certain madman had the same vision. Why is this, as well, a telling criticism of a theory which focuses only upon the personal unconscious? What is the "primordial idea" both men stumbled upon? Anticipating our reading of the essays on religion, given that these sublime ideas are there, ready to be plucked like golden apples, what is the proper role and function of authentic religion?

3. The question of morality reappears too, when Jung defines the characteristics of a personal, neurotic, condition (p. 273). Are these "moral" conflicts the products of the patient's conflict with his or her parents or other authorities whose task it is to constrain instinctual urges in others? If not, whence comes the "moral" dimension of the neurotic's suffering? And if assimilating the unconscious is tantamount to cure, upon what factors does cure depend? (Could such cures have taken place before the discovery of Freud's psychotherapeutic method?)

4. Jung says assimilating the unconscious to the ego can be extremely dangerous and lead to disaster, but also can be extremely valuable. In fact, he describes three possible outcomes. Why is each of them dependent upon a proper understanding of the *collective* dimension of the unconscious? Why could a Freudian analyst, according to Jung, not be capable of helping patients achieve an authentic relationship with their deepest unconscious?

5. There is no hint of mysticism in this essay. Indeed, why might one find that Jung was closer to biological claims and a biological psychology than was Freud? Why is the fact that human beings share a common brain an indication that, fundamentally, they share common psychological structures at a deep, indeed the deepest, level? Upon what physical model does Jung base his claims that consciousness and the personal unconscious depend upon and grow out of a substratum of unconscious, collective

"well-nigh automatic portions of the individual psyche" (p. 276)?

6. How is the fact that different anthropologists portray the same tribe in radically distinct moralistic manners, a sign of the essential bipolarity of the collective psyche? And why are members of such tribes living in a kind of paradise? Assuming Jung's description is correct, ought we to find among them the kind of neuroses which typify life in our culture?

7. Yet with differentiation from the collective comes the possibility of consciousness raised to a pinnacle point: what must be the inevitable costs of such an ascension? Recall Miss Miller: what was the price she paid for touching close to the collective which was otherwise unavailable to her? Does Jung feel that analysis pure and simple provides a safe avenue for exploring the degree to which one's consciousness rests upon the collective? Indeed, why must we avoid giving a singular answer to this question? How is it that the word person signifies "one thing to the introvert and another to the extravert" (p. 278, n.)?

8. It seems that the ideal route to psychic health is one midway between denying the collective its due (as Freud did?) and collapsing one's individuality into the collective (as who did?). Why can we not then simply identify our individuality with what appears to be uniquely us—our conscious personality (p. 281)? And why is the latter typically the product of the collective masquerading as an individual? If the persona is but a mask, how can we lift it, when to our everyday experience it appears *identical* to ourselves?

9. Yet lifting or dissolving the persona is fraught with dangers. Why would patients (and others?) experience it as if they were flying, or akin to the gods and planets, or other semi-divine or divine forces? Why would psychiatrists be well advised to read deeply in the history of religions and cultural anthropology? If Jung is correct about these dangers, what attitudes toward the persona and its unveiling must we expect most people to manifest when they approach its dissolution? Why are they wrong?

10. As he did in *Symbols of Transformation*, Jung invokes the legend of Faust, as represented in Goethe's masterpiece, in order to explicate the ego's relationship to the collective. Do these invocations work equally well for non-German readers? If not, upon which American, British or French texts might one draw in order to find similar insights about the persona and other archetypes? (Must all cultures have such texts?)

11. Jung describes two major responses to the dissolution of the persona: why is the first regressive and dangerous and the second equally dangerous? Why does Jung invoke another great German

authority, on p. 286, when he alludes to the possibility of gaining access to the "treasure" lying just out of the reach of consciousness? Why is the pathway to this treasure identical, in feeling and quality, to the tasks which confront mythical heroes like Prometheus and Siegfried? (The latter appears in full garb in MDR.)

12. Assuming Jung's analysis of the propensity toward monism in modern life is correct, what geometric or symbolic figures must we find associated with persons who have avoided the pitfalls of regression and identification with the collective? Why must we be grateful to thinkers like Bergson (and Jung himself) who are willing to defend the irrational against the claims of monists everywhere? (Would Jung's thesis find many defenders among Western university professors?)

13. After an appropriate reference to William James, whose book, *The Varieties of Religious Experience*, permeates much of Jung's thinking, Jung argues psychology cannot be scientific except to the degree it focuses upon collective phenomena. Why can there be no complete and rigorous science of the individual? (Do most people believe some part of themselves is forever unknowable by others?)

14. Jung turns to the question of fantasy and technical issues of psychotherapy. However, these are crucial elements in his general theory since they indicate how the relationship or balance between conscious and unconscious forces is to be achieved or, if lost, reconstituted in treatment. On these grounds, why are both the concrete and semiotic interpretations of fantasy wrong, if not deadly? Have we seen Jung practice the art of hermeneutics he here describes (pp. 290–291)?

15. Although they do not generally acknowledge it, many contemporary philosophers of religion promulgate theories of symbol similar to Jung's. For example, some argue that the symbol is primary to reflection, including theology. What support, from the side of clinical theory, does Jung offer to this concept? Why does he argue symbols function always as linkages between what is known and what is unknowable? How does this theorem in turn permit him to add his "objective associations" to those of his patients without danger of leading them astray?

16. In the paragraphs added by the CW editors Jung appears to champion the cause of mysticism and trivial pastimes like horoscopes and numerology. Does this mean he himself believes such exercises are accurate forms of science? If not, why should the science of psychology take them seriously? (Freud said he abjured such beliefs once his neurosis abated. Would Jung concur with this kind of cure?)

17. The term moral appears here, as it had in the previous essays. Does it suggest that psychotherapy is a kind of preaching or exhortation towards one particular point of view or single hierarchy of norms and guidelines? If so, how can we explain Jung's fierce protection of the right to be different as seen in his initial discussion of psychological types? If not, in what does this "morality" consist? Could successful treatment issue in the patient becoming less loving, less "virtuous," and less admirable than he or she was prior to analysis?

18. What constitutes a cured patient, according to the principles Jung advances here? Why ought patients to become aware of the barometric measurements their dreams send to them? And could they do so through some method other than psychoanalysis? Given Jung's basic argument in this early essay, must all cultures elaborate methods for discerning these "life-lines"? What methods were available to Western persons before the advent of Freud?

19. The addendum, pp. 295–304, is less articulate than the original paper, but equally valuable since it reveals Jung's attempt to formulate first a description of "individuality" (a topic about which Freud said very little) and the ego's relation to the fundamental archetypes, anima and animus. If the topic of individuality (and individuation) are as primary as Jung says they are, why is his work pioneering and the territory virginal?

20. If the "natural and unconscious attitude is harmonious" (p. 296), why do we find rampant neuroses among all modern peoples? More so, why does consciousness, which would seem to be the singular achievement of human beings, destabilize the original psychic matrix? Why must individuation be won only at the cost of suffering an intrusion of forces that "seems to us irrational" (p. 297)?

21. Following this excursion into logic, Jung sketches out three attempts to describe the structure of the psyche (pp. 298–304). On what grounds, with what criteria in mind, does he distinguish one "realm" or aspect from another? Examine carefully the dominant metaphors he uses in this architectonics: why is the collective unconscious the *innermost core*?

22. As the CW editors note, Jung's struggle to clarify his concepts in this early text bore fruit much later in his widely respected essay, *Psychological Types* (1921, CW 6). To comprehend fully his mature thought one should read that study. Thanks to the publication of MDR we know that this essay is more than an exercise in metapsychology; it describes his own struggles with the collective as well. One of his intellectual struggles is to find a vocabulary suitable to his discoveries. For example, he says the ego may

ego may identify with the persona or with the anima. How can this be if the ego is defined—as he later proposed—as precisely that entity circumscribed by consciousness?

23. In a similar way, what larger model of the psyche must he have in mind when he says some persons fear "reality" as much as normals fear the unconscious (p. 300)?

24. Although they are condensed, the two versions of the conclusion are worth careful consideration and comparison. (Photocopying these pages and comparing one version against the other facilitates this task.) Jung appears to have labored over the sections on individuality and the collective unconscious. In version one he says there are insufficient criteria with which to determine whether or not a given psychological product is collective or the opposite. What are the criteria he proposes in version two? Why must collective contents be projected onto external objects? (If this is so, what is the task of analytic treatment?) Where have we seen "primordial images" in the case of Miss Miller and other persons about whom Jung has written?

IV
PSYCHOLOGY OF RELIGION
Psychology and Religion (1938) CW 11
"A Psychological Approach to the Trinity" (1942) CW 11
"Transformation Symbolism in the Mass" (1942) CW 11
"On Synchronicity" (1952) CW 8
Aion: Researches Into the Phenomenology of the Self (1951)
CW 9.2
Answer to Job (1952) CW 11

As mentioned in the introduction to this study, given a severe page limitation we cannot read all of Jung's major texts. We might well consider his famous essay on psychological types (comprising all of CW 6), his many works on alchemy (in CW 12, 13, and 14), and his essays on individual archetypes (in CW 9, part 1, and CW 10). But since our major concern is to develop a critical understanding of his theory of religion, we turn to those essays which are most directly concerned with it in its Western forms. Although he esteemed highly Eastern thought, Jung's comments on it derive from his more fundamental works on Western forms of spirituality. Because we have developed systematically his major claims and worked through his basic model of the psyche, we can read these applied essays a great deal more rapidly and easily than the texts we considered initially. Hence, while the reading may appear lengthy, our speed can increase correspondingly.

Psychology and Religion (1938) CW 11

Technical Terms

Phenomenology; *numinosum*; *religio*; *pistis*; dogma; quaternity; *rontundum*.

"The Autonomy of the Unconscious" (pp. 5–33)

We read this essay because it represents Jung's first public pronouncements upon the relationship between his psychological theory and traditional religious concerns. However, beginning with his dissertation on the occult, Jung was involved deeply with issues of religious experience and belief. More so, as occurs with other works, this 1938 essay has its roots in an earlier piece, "Dream Symbols and the Process of Individuation" published in 1935. It was later added to one of his volumes on alchemy where it appears as "Individual Dream Symbolism in Relation to Alchemy" (CW 12).

1. Why should scholars of religion pay attention to the *consensus gentium* when other scientists and researchers may safely ignore the folklore, fantasy, and nonsensical notions which make up ordinary opinions about complex matters of nature? Why does the phenomenology of religion require us to accept these naive assertions? Why is the numinosum always experienced as exterior to oneself?

2. After referring to William James, whose *The Varieties of Religious Experience* (1902) is a comrade worthy of Jung's essays, Jung defines religion as an attitude. Why is this attitude prior to belief (or *pistis*)? Why are those who ridicule dogma as being merely assertions designed to kill the spirit wrong? If dogma "lives" and changes through time yet is always essentially the same, to what level of the psyche must we assign its origins?

3. Modern medicine (including Freud?) abjures the belief in spirits and seeks always for the biological source of disease. Modern patients reluctantly speak of their neuroses as if these psychical disorders were like actual maladies, yet, at the same time, they reduce them to the merely imaginary. Why are neurotic disorders as real and as "cancerous" as the neurotic fears them to be? (Are religious beliefs as real and dangerous as neurotic disorders?)

4. Jung reverts back to issues raised by the WAT; how do unconscious complexes "answer" or respond to stimulus words apart from any intervention by the conscious mind? This raises again the question of how Jung differs fundamentally from Freud on the question of the ego (or conscious mind) and its responsibility for unconscious contents. Could Freud ever agree with Jung's statement, "It is just as if the complex were an autonomous being" (p. 13)? If not, could Freud ever agree to Jung's positive evaluation of "numinous" messages from the unconscious?

5. What strengths does Jung grant to human reason and intellect when faced with upsurges in unconscious, volcanic, materials? Why is it not adequate, according to Jung's basic model of the psyche, to inform patients that, somehow, they are responsible for their symptoms, even the cancerous ones of which they are most afraid? In the same way, why does he find the story of Gilgamesh especially instructive for contemporary psychotherapists?

6. Jung turns to the major topic of his essay: how can one distinguish

great, archetypal dreams from ordinary dreams? He quotes at length from Christian authorities (pp. 19–21). How do religious experts distinguish between visions and communications sent them by good spirits and those sent them by evil spirits, who, as is well known, may masquerade themselves in the garb and tone of the former? Does Jung himself agree that only a certain rigorous doctrinal stand will authorize one to interpret great dreams correctly? If not, what criteria does he advance for making what is evidently a major distinction?

7.   To illustrate his theory of dreams, and by extension his essential psychology of religion, Jung describes in brief some dreams of a patient upon whom he reported at length in the 1935 essay on dreams and individuation (reprinted in the Princeton text on dreams). How do his dreams reveal the separate and independent existence of an unconscious which attempts to compensate for errors or exaggerations of consciousness? Which of the dream elements are products of a collective mind and a collective, national, spirit, and which are products of the dreamer's individual experience?

8.   Assuming Jung's judgment about the female character is correct (p. 29) and given the theory of individuation advanced in his essay of 1916, at which point in this man's treatment must this dream have occurred? On what grounds does Jung add to the patient's associations his own reflections, plus associations and dreams from other patients? In other words, what basic principle justifies a collective form of dream interpretation as it did Jung's method in *Symbols of Transformation*?

9.   The anima archetype is linked both to animosity and to the male's physiological status (pp. 30–31). How, in turn, does Jung link these facts to the seemingly disparate mythologems which explain the birth of one kind of woman out of man's side, as Eve was born from Adam? Is the anima's speech a product of a wholly distinct "sub-personality," whose character is undetermined by the patient's actual life circumstances?

10. Although the church dream conveys a frivolous and superficial attitude toward religion, of which the dreamer had very low opinions, Jung says it is not insignificant for those reasons. Once it is seen as a response to deeper themes, expressed in the dreams which precede and follow it, we can see the true depths of the patient's religious concerns. Why would the patient dream of gibbons and the transformation of animals into human beings? In the spirit of collective interpretation, what associations do these "theriomorphic" ideas arouse? What *phylogenetic* rationale do the dreams manifest?

11. In "Dogma and Natural Symbols," chapter two, Jung mounts a

vivid and passionate defense of theological dogma and a vivid and heartfelt attack on modern rationalism and mediocre intellectuals. Why was his patient, a scientist, terrified of dream-images, which were common parlance two thousand years ago?

12. Jung reports another dream (pp. 35–36) in which a voice is heard announcing certain moral truths. Are such voices typical of dreams? Is the dream itself "dream-like" in the ordinary sense of that term? If not, what style or form does it manifest? What is its tone and language? As before, Jung adduces additional associations from his own vast learning. Assuming this is legitimate, how would the dreamer respond to this kind of amplification (assuming Jung might convey it to him)?

13. "There can be no doubt that is a basic religious phenomenon" (p. 39). Why? Where else have we seen Jung take issue with those who would claim such voices are merely the dreamer's thoughts expressed under a convenient guise? Why is the unconscious mind not merely *my* mind? Yet such voices issue from a center—but not one which is "identical with the conscious ego" (p. 40). Does this mean the unconscious center (later identified with the archetype of the self) is necessarily distinct and other than one's conscious ego? In whom might we expect to find an amalgamation of both centers into a complete and enduring whole?

14. Jung would appear to be wholly in favor of religion, however vaguely one defines it; yet, on pp. 42ff., he seems to distinguish between a healthy, liberating form, and a traditional "creedal" form. (Jumping ahead to MDR, to which branch would his father, a Protestant pastor, have belonged?) How did the traditional Catholic Church protect its members against both psychic collapse and direct religious experience?

15. Is Jung critical of this "Catholic defense" (p. 45)? Or did the Catholic defense work well at one time, and for reasons beyond the Church's control, lose its efficacy in the modern period? Yet dogma, Jung seems to say, is infinitely more alive and valuable than mere rationalism. Why are the rapidity of scientific advance, and the scientific distrust of metaphor and symbols, precisely elements that count against its enduring value for human self-understanding and happiness?

16. Jung does not hestitate to make claims about the shape of Western history. For example, how does he trace the rise of modern Western science to the triumph of Protestantism in northern Europe? (Compare Max Weber's famous treatise on a similar issue, *The Protestant Ethic and the Spirit of Capitalism* [1904/5]). Is Jung's description of international paranoid mechanisms entirely beside the point in contemporary international politics? How do Soviet

and American politicians, for example, portray life and times in the land of the other?

17. Jung develops the concept archetype along a new line, explains its genetic source, and then explicates the image of the four candles and the quaternity archetype which has been suppressed in the West. If Jung is correct, and given his theory that the psyche seeks equilibrium, what *must* we expect to find in contemporary religiosity? How will these new religious dynamics appear in and influence the dreams of even his most naive and rationalistic patients? (Why does Jung say number symbolism has a venerable history [p. 52]?)

18. His patient, who had recorded most of his dreams prior to seeing Jung, reports images and ideas which were conscious knowledge a few hundred years before, and the core of religious dogma a few thousand years before that. How can we account for this shift in the degree to which the ego has access to what were once conscious, and therefore potentiated, symbols? How had the latter kept the powers of hell chained up and so prevented the outbreak of mass psychoses, like the first World War? (How would Jung explain this remarkable title?)

19. "But why should my patient recapitulate these old speculations?" (p. 57) is precisely the question at issue. Alchemy is a despised "pseudo-science" as are numerology and astrology. Yet Jung continually finds them valuable resources for his investigations. Why? In fact, why is the degree to which moderns despise these ancient sciences a measure of their own lack of insight? Why are they cut off from perceiving the "life-producing sun in the depths of the unconscious" (p. 58)? (What kind of sun could inhabit the unconscious? With what qualities of light or shade is the unconscious usually associated?)

20. From the patient's many dreams in which the quaternity symbol appears on its own accord, Jung argues that the ancient dogma of the Trinity, a central facet of the Church's teaching, cannot remain unchallenged. What is the voice of nature that challenges the hegemony of the Trinity in Christian speculation? If it is a natural tendency, can theology pretend to dissuade it? Why did official theology obscure what Jung finds everywhere revealed in the dreams of his modern and enlightened patients? Where else have we seen Jung describe something as "an autonomous personality" (p. 59) with freedom and eternality?

21. In the final pages of this section Jung adds yet another dimension to the Trinity: *to somaton*, which means earth or body. Why is this aspect of the collective unconscious and therefore another dimension of the divine, as repressed and as denied as was the

shadow? Jung composed this essay in 1937. In 1950 the Catholic
Church raised Mary to the status of Queen of Heaven (see CW
11, p. 171,n). Why would Jung take the latter as a confirmation of
his fundamental views? (We consider this point at length below
when we read his essay on the Trinity and his long piece on Job.)

22. In the third section of this essay, Jung describes what he claims is
the patient's most important vision. On what grounds can he
argue this point? Why in fact does Jung call it a conversion? (If
these are archetypal elements in the patient's dreams, what must
we expect to find in dreams of patients who are equally advanced
in the process of individuation? Jung gives us one example: is this
sufficient to convince all skeptics? With what rationale could Jung
himself have accepted it with so much certitude?)

23. After presenting his patient's dream-vision Jung notes that the
feeling of sublime harmony is especially difficult to explain. Why
is the patient's feeling of utmost importance in ascertaining the
degree to which a dream or vision or other artifact is archetypal?
As with other such artifacts Jung adds to the patient's associations
his own, far vaster and more learned associations drawn from
classical literature and arcane subjects. Yet even these are not
sufficiently alike since the center in the dream-vision is empty
(p. 67). Luckily, Jung reports, he found a much closer replica in a
fourteenth-century poem. Why was he so lucky?

24. In the same way why does Jung feel confident enough to assert
that the missing fourth color is obviously blue, and from this fact
deduce the central claim that the poet's concerns and Jung's
patient's (and Jung's) are identical: the divine status of Mary
(p. 71)? How does this dream-vision, like the poem, solve the age-
old puzzle of the relationship between unlike substances, like matter and psyche, or god and human, or principles like mortality
and immortality?

25. How are these in turn linked to classic philosophic conundrums
like squaring the circle, perpetual motion, and the like (pp. 72–
73)? Yet if Jung is correct about the depth of these solutions, why
were they not more universally acknowledged? If in fact his
patient and the medieval poet envisioned an adequate solution to
these deeply disturbing puzzles, why did the Church and philosophy proper not retain them? In the same way, if the quaternity is
an archetypal entity, why is it "entirely absent from the dogma"
(p. 73) if dogma is the living expression of archetypal elements?

26. Freud is often labeled a mechanist who failed to comprehend the
depths of existential freedom inherent in human life. Is Jung's theory entirely devoid of mechanical or automatic schemata? If so,
how shall one understand the sureness with which he can (1) predict

the elements missing from his patient's dreams, and (2) explain why his patient's dreams change, "astonishingly enough" (p. 75), when the patient resists insight into the archetypal nature of his visions?

27. The issue of the patient's religiosity and his specific Christian identity arises anew when Jung makes the remarkable statement that at the center of the patient's mandala "we find no trace of a deity . . . but, on the contrary, a mechanism" (p. 80). In fact, Jung says, in most patients one finds no deity at the center of their mandalas. Why does Jung nevertheless feel such visions are religious and that that factor which instantiates the greatest power is rightly called "God" (p. 81)? When questioned, such patients describe experiences which Jung says are "almost like what used to be expressed by saying: He has made his peace with God" (pp. 81–82). Is this close enough to a Christian or Jewish understanding to identify these therapeutic experiences with religious experiences? What or Who is at the center of human existence according to either Jewish or Christian beliefs? (On the issue of mechanisms and self-identity see Victor Tausk's famous work, "On the Origin of the 'Influencing Machine' in Schizophrenia" [*Psychoanalytic Quarterly*, 2:519-556, 1933].)

28. Jung would appear to champion gnostic, alchemical, and other traditions about which official religion has always been suspicious, or downright hostile. Is his emphasis upon the emptiness of the mandala's center compatible with current Christian (or Jewish teachings)? Will it ever be compatible with them? If yes, why have official religions been so slow to see the truth? If no, why do Jung's patients choose a path apart from the wide road offered them by traditional religion? Another way of putting this question is to ask why Nietzsche was both completely modern and yet tragic (pp. 85–87)?

29. Thomas Jefferson studied the New Testament carefully and then with scissors and paste edited it according to the lines he felt a gospel should have. (Sue Bridehead does the same in Thomas Hardy's tragedy, *Jude the Obscure*.) How would Jung explain these efforts at reconstruction? Are there parallels in contemporary scientific study of religion? Would devout Christians find the center of their mandalas empty or inhabited by a mechanism, or would they find something else? And, looking ahead to our reading of MDR, what did Jung find when he ventured forth on his own journey of self-discovery? And for whom does he write these texts?

30. Jung says he takes these ancient dogmas and and pours them "into moulds of immediate experience" (p. 89). What small and great factors condition what he calls immediate experience? While he discusses timeless characteristics of myths and the unconscious,

does he rely upon or formulate a theory of history per se? Recall our discussion of the formulation of creeds: were they bound up with particular historical epochs as well? Yet Jung prefers to quote from the alchemists, e.g., "Transform yourself into living philosophical stones!" (p. 94). Why?

31. Jung is perfectly aware that Gnosticism, like the other arcane subjects which he finds his patient's dreams recapitulate naively and automatically, is heresy according to traditional Christian norms. In fact, why does this account for their resurrection in modern peoples, most of whom have no knowledge of these historical roots? Why does Jung not refer to contemporary Christian theologians or other religious authorities when he makes these broad generalizations about the state of modern religious life?

32. After describing another patient's archetypal dream, Jung returns to the question of the source of these symbols and their meaning. How important is his contention that most of his patients had no knowledge of any of the alchemical treatises and other arcana to which he found so many parallels? What kinds of empirical studies or tests would one want to conduct before accepting or championing Jung's claims? (For example, might his patients have read some of his many publications prior to visiting him for psychotherapy? Or might they have picked up subtle clues from his office, or his demeanor when such topics were touched upon, or might he himself have created confirming instances when he focused upon archetypal themes?)

33. "Religious experience is absolute; it cannot be disputed" (p. 104). What does this mean in this context and in general for the possibility of a psychology of religion? What kinds of experience can be disputed? If none can be, how is religion any different? If most can be, what distinguishes the majority from *religious* experience? Is the amount of splendor and help a belief offers one a measure of its truth-value? (According to whom? To what American philosophic tradition could Jung appeal for justification of his fundamental metaphysics?)

"A Psychological Approach to the Dogma of the Trinity" (1942) CW 11

Most readers will find this and the following essays especially difficult. Jung deals with texts which range from Babylonian hymns and Egyptian thanatology to the early Church fathers, Plato, and Gnostic and alchemical treatises. As rich and as fascinating as these subjects are, I do not focus upon them in these questions. I wish to raise issues and questions about the logic of Jung's method and the ways in which he advances his basic ideas. In addition, the latter sections of his essay contain succinct statements of his fundamental theorems about archetypes and lead us to consider his final works on religion and the question of God's repressed characteristics: his femininity and his darkness. (Regarding his historical and technical claims, I refer to the texts listed in the appendix to this work.)

1. Jung says the notion of a triad of gods is an archetype in the history of religions. While he cites pre-Christian religious parallels to the doctrine of the Trinity, does he grant to each equal dignity and as it were power? If not, on what grounds can the psychologist of religion distinguish the values of one formulation over another? If they are equal, how can we account for the development or at least change which appears to have taken place as Egyptian beliefs gave way to Christian? (Must "later" always equal "more advanced"?) If archetypes are everywhere the same and believed by all and full of numinous power (p. 117), how could some peoples have a deeper or better grasp of them than others?

2. In his condensed discussion of Greek metaphysics and numerology Jung suggests the equilateral triangle is a conceptual "model for the logical image of the Trinity" (p. 119). From there Jung links up his own theories of archetypal images and from there his notion of characterology (p. 121). Are these latter theorems about the relationship between thinking and feeling, for example, merely conceptual models as well? Does Jung believe his theorems about the psyche's quadrilateral structure permit him to *predict* a particular person's behavior? And do they also allow him to predict a particular culture's behavior? (Cf. above his "The Role of the Unconscious" [1918]).

3. This question returns to us when we examine Jung's diagrams of Plato's speculations (pp. 125–128), particularly the plan of the village on p. 127. As we will see in MDR Jung himself had such a vision in a "great dream" he had at the end of his confrontation with the unconscious: passing through the Alley of the Dead he sees a fountain of light within a city square surrounded by circular streets. Jung does not mention this vision, which predates this essay by more than thirty years. Is a *"spiritus rector"* responsible for this interesting conjunction as well?

4. In the second section we read that "the archetype reasserted itself" (p. 130). What does this mean? Having discussed Plato at length, Jung concludes that we need not assume he influenced the Church's trinitarian ideas in any way. Then what did give rise to the latter? Similarly, we learn that the Holy Ghost is not a logical datum but an archetypal one. If so, and if the archetypes are the forms of the instincts, that is archaic or primordial forms out of which religion

and metaphysics draw their substance, where are the female elements which we saw so distinctly in *Symbols of Transformation*?

5. Although he finds no explicit evidence for trinitarian formulae within the New Testament, Jung holds there are clear signs the archetype is there "throwing up triadic formations" (p. 139). How does Jung understand the development of the creeds he describes in this chapter? Given his overall argument, to what does he ascribe the motive force and power behind the alterations in the creedal statements? And why would this alteration, if occurring as he describes, require centuries upon centuries to mature fully? Again, which elements here discussed are the most active and responsible for the appearance of fundamental Christian doctrines?

6. This chapter, "The Problem of the Fourth," will prove difficult to those who have not read Jung's essay on psychological types (CW 6, also in *Portable Jung*). He begins with one of his favorite quotations from Goethe about the fourth who would not come. How is this obscure line linked, according to Jung, to the fourfold structure of the psychic functions?

7. The inferior function may not be unconscious, yet it is typically experienced as if it were an intruder. Why is this so, and why would it appear to be autonomous, driven, and obsessive? Primitives, we are told, recognize the importance of this fourth, while moderns tend to ignore it, at their peril. Why is the West particularly apt to forget these inferior functions and, given Jung's opinions about its instinctual origins, why would our culture repress knowledge of its existence? (And how would it treat those who uncover it once more?)

8. The theme of cultural repression takes on special urgency for Jung when he addresses, again, the problem of evil, and the *absence* of a female deity in the West. How, in fact, is each figure a "fourth" whose divinity has not yet been recognized fully? As we saw in his 1918 essay on politics, Jung feels his general theory of archetypes and their ineluctable return from the repressed allows him to predict the overall shape of Western spirituality. How does the dogma of the *Assumptio Mariae*, promulgated in 1950, serve to verify his overall claims? And how is the latter itself prefigured in Plato's speculations on the fourth as well?

9. Does Jung argue for a theory of the psyche based upon his readings of religious history, or does he generate a theory of religion based upon his study of psychology? In other words, does he claim his analysis of trinities and quaternities reflects an exhaustive, inductive survey? Of the many similarities he uncovers, between Plato, early Christian speculations, and alchemy, are any causally related to one another? If not, how does he account for

their uncanny similarities? *What* produces these "preconscious, prefigurative connections" (p. 174)?

10. Throughout this chapter Jung seems to argue two points of view: one is logical, the other psychological. Logically he seems to link the necessity of evil with the semantic pairs, light-dark, high-low, and so on. Psychologically he suggests a well-balanced psyche (and a well-balanced culture) require one to give adequate attention to polar opposites, like good and evil. Is this the whole of his argument? If so, why does he contrast Pythagorean beliefs with Christian theology? How is the latter a moral and religious advance over the former?

11. But has the official Church recognized these facts as clearly as it should? (This raises again the issue of Jung's relationship to orthodox Christian teachings: if the latter are wrong systematically according to analytical psychology, can the Church, in return, accept fully Jung's teachings?) Can the Church agree that the Trinity and Quaternity are products of an age-old process within the psyche which *projects* out into nature its internal workings?

12. In part ii, "The Psychology of the Quarternity," Jung returns to the question of the development of personality and its relationship to religious history. How does he link the development of trinitarian theology with the corresponding development of an individual's psyche? Given his biological understanding of the archetypes, ought all religions to manifest similar developments of their primary symbols? Can there be any single revelation complete and sufficient unto itself?

13. How does Christ's crucifixion between two criminals foreshadow the psyche's agony in its own birthing? From the Father, to the Son, to the Spirit marks one sequence of religious maturation: is it also the sequence for personal maturation? What lies beyond these three figures? And, returning to an earlier question, why is the fourth typically not represented by a *personal* entity (p. 185)? Does everyone wish to achieve a state of "adamantine stability" (p. 186)? Does everyone who contemplates his or her fate share this value as well as Jung's enthusiasm for seeing deep similarities between photons and the Holy Ghost (p. 187)?

14. In part iii, "General Remarks on Symbolism," Jung summarizes his theory of symbols and gives us glimpses of his psychotherapeutic methods. Why can symbols not be made to order? Having just read about the numinosity associated with archetypal symbols, we are surprised to discover that trinitarian and quaternity symbols appear "very banal" (p. 189) from the outside. If they are to serve individuation, what must occur, at some point, in one's experience of them?

15. Is psychotherapy essentially unlike religious education? If Jung's fundamental claim about the archetypes is correct, can his patients avoid "fear and trembling" when they enter into a direct confrontation with collective unconscious contents? Since all religions are expressions and elaborations of the archetypes, and since Christianity has long dominated Western religiosity, why is it not sufficient for modern persons? Another way of asking this, from Jung's point of view, is what historical factors have produced analytical psychology itself? What role does it play in the maturation of Western spirituality?

16. Before reaching the "Conclusion," Jung summarizes his understanding of the Trinity—and points out the importance of the Mass in the development of Western religiosity. Sometimes the Mass is undeniably effective; other times it fails (p. 192). Are these latter occasions instances of moral errors? If not, why do some people perceive the Mass's archetypal richness, while others see nothing but ancient customs and archaic beliefs? Why is Catholicism more likely to effect personal transformations than is Protestantism? Did Jung's patients, or SW or Miss Miller, find recourse to Christianity, or did Christianity fail them in some way? Did it also fail the alchemists about whom Jung wrote so much?

17. Jung's theory of symbols is tied directly to his theory of the archetypes. If the latter are real entities, shaped by their origins in the dispositions of fundamental instincts, what is the ontological status of their products, symbols? When Jung writes of the power certain symbols may exert upon the psyche, is he being metaphorical and poetic? If so, how can he say also that not handling certain symbols correctly can lead to disastrous psychic consequences? If archetypical symbols are merely metaphorical in their origins, how can Jung predict with aplomb the future consequence of a culture's repressing certain key archetypal representatives?

18. The distinction between symbol, artifact, and metaphor reappears in Jung's writings on technique. But even in this essay we read that appearances of quaternities, no matter how banal, are "like shadow pictures of important things" (p. 189). What are these important things? Are they substantial in some way, or are they merely the result of particular kinds of speculation of particular philosophers in particular cultures? If the latter, how can Jung assert with his customary authority that they appear everywhere and always as essentially the same? But these important things have their own natural history as well: why does Jung agree with the Church's historic claim to evaluate the source of spiritual revelations (p. 195)?

19. The world-soul, according to Plato and Jung, is necessarily

incomplete. Why does this argue in favor of trinitarian conceptions of the Godhead? Had God not done so, Jung tells us, the world would be little more than a perfect "machine, and then the incarnation and the redemption would never have come about" (p. 196). Why does this follow? If the addition of the fourth constitutes harmony and therefore stasis, does the corresponding process within psychotherapy-individuation also constitute a state of machine-like regularity? Is it also a state of "absolute totality" (p. 196)?

20. Does Jung himself believe straightforwardly the dogmas with which he is concerned in this text? If not, on what ground does he argue for their validity? Would medieval Christians have understood that argument? Why can modern, sophisticated, persons ill-afford to overlook these apparently lifeless disputes over the Trinity and its theological justifications? Can the *consensus omnium* be wrong at any point? (Are there other medieval beliefs which seem absolutely wrong to us now? Would anyone now justify the slaughter of witches that preoccupied many learned minds for many, many years?)

21. Related to this question is a general problem Jung raised in his initial rejection of Freud's psychology. That is, Freud sought to explain the source and meaning of both neurotic symptoms and cultural institutions, particularly religion. For by explaining their origins one could hope to remove both the symptom and its cultural counterparts, irrational religious beliefs. How does Jung's adherence to the theory of archetypes permit him to claim both a general scientific status for his work and to affirm the possibility that Catholicism is, in fact, true? We see this question reappear in his detailed consideration of the central Christian ritual, the Mass.

"Transformation Symbolism in the Mass" (1942) CW 11

Technical Terms

Symbol; natural symbols; miracle; individuation; *participation mystique*; enantiodromia; mandala; quaternity.

The topic of the Mass and the process of transubstantiation, by which the mundane wine and bread are converted into the sacred body and blood of Christ, is a natural object for Jung's analytical scrutiny. Indeed, given the central concerns of his *Symbols of Transformation*, it is surprising that he waited thirty years to address this fundamental Christian ritual. By the time he did so he had elaborated the whole of his own theory. Consequently, we may read it quickly and pay special attention to the question which circles around it: what distinguishes the

Mass from the savage rites which resemble it?

1. Jung conveniently divides up the essay into four parts. The first
    two are descriptive and technical. We focus on the latter two in
    which he applies his theory to the Mass. Yet we might ponder his
    first sentence: if this is true, in some sense, is analytical psychology
    a proper approach? Jung disowns any trace of mockery or disdain
    (indeed, he says a number of times quite the opposite). That is not
    the question. The question is, can one use a theory derived from
    the study of fragmenting personalities to explicate a "still living
    mystery"?

2. The theme of mystery returns when Jung distinguishes between
    the theological concepts of mystery and symbol (p. 207). How
    does the Mass as a *symbol* coexist with the mystery of Christ's
    presence? At the same time, on what grounds does Jung say that
    Christ's appearance in the Mass at the moment of consecration is
    a revelation of something existing for all time beyond the bounds
    of space and time? What features of the analytic patient's experi-
    ences are also "beyond the power of man to conceive" (p. 207)?
    Can we conclude that what is beyond the patient is identical to
    the beyond to which the Mass points as theological symbol? In
    other words, are the mysteries of the archetypes identical to those
    of Catholicism or merely similar to them?

3. In his summary of the sequence of the transformation Jung points
    repeatedly to parallels between it and alchemical treatises (e.g.,
    p. 209). Are the latter identical in substance as well as form to the
    former? Consider the prayer on p. 211: it ends with a description
    of Jesus' partaking of our humanity. Is this emphasis upon his
    human qualities identical to the alchemical goal of magical trans-
    formation of self and acquisition of immortality? Do alchemical
    treatises avoid being more than "common magic" (p. 215)?

4. In his conclusion Jung summarizes his description of the Mass's
    sequences and notes that the masculine wine and the feminine
    bread correspond to the male and female believers who make up
    the body of the Church. And these in turn are represented in the
    androgynous nature of Christ (p. 221). How can we account for
    these parallels? Must an authentic religion (assuming there may
    be more than one) reflect such parallels automatically? Are these
    then theological requirements? Can analytical principles help us
    assess the value of one theology over another? (Would this, in
    turn, help the historian explain why some beliefs became official
    dogma, while others became despised heresies?)

5. In the third part, Jung describes numerous non-Christian rituals
    which parallel some aspect or another of the Mass. Chief of these are

human sacrifice and eating human beings. Would most unsophisticated Christians find these parallels of major interest and aids toward deepening their faith? If not, how would Jung justify, indeed, champion the importance of seeing how pervasive these ideas are? We assume the Aztecs had no inkling of the Mass, yet their major rites are strikingly similar to it. Does this detract or enhance the believer's feelings about the Mass? (Why were the Spanish fathers upset by their discovery of these Aztec ceremonies?)

6. This question reappears when we consider Jung's discussion of the visions of Zosimos (pp. 226ff). What are the major feeling tones of the latter's vision? Are these identical to the feelings which pervade the Mass, or any New Testament descriptions of Jesus' sufferings? Jung says alchemists like Zosimos were even threatened with insanity. What would distinguish, in Jung's mind, someone who is merely threatened with insanity from someone who is actually insane? Miss Miller, in *Symbols of Transformation*, also had a vision of a sacrifice. It was overwhelming to her; are most Christians overwhelmed by the Mass? (Or should they be—according to Jung?)

7. That Mercury is related to the concept "spirit" is, Jung says, an "ancient astrological fact" (p. 233). What weight is he giving to this latter term? When we learn that the alchemists looked to Mercury as their saviour and mediator (pp. 234–235), does this require us to see a fundamental identity between them and the orthodox theology of the Mass? Are the transformations of blood into semen and milk (p. 237) identical in form and content to the transformation of the wafer and the wine in the Mass? How literally does Jung appear to take these recipes for magical potions and spells?

8. The blood and guts flow a great deal faster in the descriptions which follow, e.g., the "head mysteries" to which Jung ascribes a twelfth-century midrash about the teraphim. Midst these descriptions Jung inserts a radical claim about the rise of modern consciousness and, paradoxically, the rise of modern unconsciousness. Why did the depersonalization of nature and the triumph of rationalism force modern peoples to conceive of an unconscious psyche? If Jung is correct, does that mean we should not find in archaic authors any recognition of either the Freudian or the Jungian unconscious? (Why did Freud then draw upon Sophocles when he chose to designate the central conflict of childhood the oedipus complex?)

"The Psychology of the Mass"

9. In part four Jung addresses himself to a scientific understanding of the Mass. How is this possible unless one can judge the accuracy of the religious propositions which both priest and participant appear to make about the Mass's meaning? Why can no one judge accurately the Church's claims about the Mass? Yet what permits psychologists to assess its meanings? Does Jung argue that the Church's own interpretations are like scientific hypotheses which are necessarily subject to revision?

10. After summarizing his reading of the official doctrine of the Mass (pp. 248–249) Jung says one must guard against proposals which make the Mass a magical action, initiated by human agents. How does the Church itself recognize this danger and deal with it? How would Jung, in turn, account for the autonomy and power which the Church ascribes to the Mass and to Christ (as part of the Godhead) working through it? What elements in the psyche are, according to Analytical Psychology, themselves autonomous and act upon the conscious ego as a numinous and powerful external force?

11. To rationalists religions are especially peculiar in that they advance claims which are inherently contradictory and logically false. Why does Jung feel these are therefore precisely indicators of their value and relevance to deep psychological experiences? How is the claim that Christ is both the agent, the sacrificer, and the victim, the sacrificed, in the Mass a *sign* of the Mass's validity? And how does this doctrine, in turn, prevent the rite from degrading into mere magic and incantation?

12. On what grounds does Jung claim that the bread and wine offered up in the Mass represent portions of the human psyche? Are these claims irreconcilable with alternative interpretations of the meaning of these symbols? (Can one state exhaustively the entire meaning of any symbol?)

13. "Nobody can give what he has not got" (p. 257). What work does this truism accomplish for Jung in his reflections on the sacrifice which animates the Mass? Did Miss Miller also sacrifice a part of herself when she articulated her fantasies about the Indian hero and his heroic struggles? If not, are there religious differences between her individual struggle and the institution of the Mass which would account for the difference between her fate— extreme mental distress—and that of most believers?

14. Jung advances his most concrete proposals on pp. 258–259 when he compares the process of individuation with the transformations of substances evident in the Mass. Many people would consider their conscious personalities to be their most individual part of

themselves. Why, according to Jung, are they wrong? In fact, why is individuation precisely that process by which the ego comes to see how deeply it relies upon profound "sub-personalities" which appear to it as autonomous and very powerful entities?

15. The "self" is not identical with consciousness, nor with the collective, yet it must emerge if the individual is to enjoy individuation. Many of Jung's statements appear to be contradictory: why is this not an overwhelming argument against their correctness? Why is he content to describe the ego *opposing* the self (p. 260)? Does this mean human beings are fundamentally split asunder at some deep level? (Are there elements in Christian doctrine which would support this kind of anthropology? Does the Church also conceive of human beings as unions of opposites?)

16. Alchemists, Gnostics, the Church Fathers, and analytical psychologists all understand one thing: salvation cannot be achieved by conscious means alone. Then what is the role of consciousness and conscious, willful acts in general? Can individuation occur spontaneously, without the intervention or aid of any conscious labor and intentions? If the self is not identical to consciousness (p. 264), how will one, consciously, experience it? Why would it appear to be timeless, ageless, and completely unlike one's ordinary notion of persons?

17. Returning to the vision of Zosimos, Jung notes that it is particularly gruesome and, when compared to the sublime form of the Mass, rude and ugly. Why then make these comparisons at all? Why does Jung feel that his work advances and champions the possibility of a reasonable Christian theology?

18. "God's guilt" is a theme which does not appear in official Church opinions, yet Jung argues we cannot avoid concluding that the idea is present, no matter how repressed or covered over. From what sources and on what ground does he argue this? How, in fact, does the vision of Zosimos help him complete the official Church's explication of Christ's sacrifice? Indeed, how does Jung link together the Mass, Zosimos's vision, animal sacrifice, and shamanistic psychotic-like experiences (p. 272)? (Given these links what kinds of experiences ought one to expect Jung's patients to undergo in their analysis with him?)

19. We note again that when Jung wishes to compare his theory of individuation with the teachings of Christians, he frequently avers not to the official Church but either to heretical or apocryphal writings (e.g., p. 273). If the archetype theory is correct and universally applicable, and if individuation is the actual process advanced by the Mass, why did the official Church not recognize it as clearly as the heretics did (and do) (see p. 279)?

20. The alchemists refer to Mercurius as the One, while Christians refer to Christ as the Mediator and as the Being in whom all things come together. How does the theorem of the collective unconscious unify these distinct ideas and place them on a *biological* foundation?

21. Jung returns to these ideas at length in *Aion*, which we consider below. However, the equation of self with Christ is nowhere better illustrated than on these pages (274-282), where Jung translates Gnostic sayings into psychological theorems. For example, how is the self an invisible light to all those who perceive it (p. 280)? And how does the self in the center *will* its own suffering, just as Christ willed his suffering (or as God willed God's self to be punished through God's Son?)

22. The difference between official Christian teachings and the speculations of the Gnostics reappears when Jung terms the latter meditations upon *natural symbols* (p. 285). How does the equation of Christ's cross with the four-sided mandala reinforce this distinction? Yet the Church refused to sanction such beliefs (or insights): why was it correct in doing so, at least in the earliest period?

23. Students and others new to Jung frequently wish to know exactly how many archetypes there are in the collective unconscious, just as anatomy students wish to know how many bones there are in the normal body. While Jung delineates the features of a number of archetypes, like the persona, anima, shadow, and self, why is it in principle impossible to count the total number? Indeed, why is it equally fair to say there is but one archetype (pp. 288–89)? Why was it left to modern consciousness, and thinkers of this century, to discover that what the Gnostics thought was a world of spirits is equally a world of physical objects?

24. While the Mass is the finest expression of Christian reflection on salvation and sacrifice, its theological foundations, laid in rationalistic philosophies, are shaky. Why would a return to Gnostic insights, at this time, serve modern peoples better than more and more clever rationalisms? And how is Analytical Psychology itself a product of a universal effort at psychic compensation which aims at retrieving the truths of the original Christian witness?

"On Synchronicity" (1952) CW 8
Portable Jung (pp. 505–518)

Technical Terms

Synchronicity; mantic signs.

This brief essay summarizes portions of Jung's monograph on the same topic (pp. 419–519 in CW 8). While the longer essay conveys his argument in more detail and, not accidently, describes his indebtedness to Arthur Schopenhauer, this short version lays out the basic concept. We will see it developed at length in *Aion*, where he compares astrological events in the first century with the synchronous appearance of Christ.

1. The first thing to note about this essay is Jung's apparent contradiction. He wishes to speak of a principle which connects one event to another (either simultaneously or otherwise) but not causally. Since this appears impossible to most rationalists, he gives a couple of examples of synchronic events from his life and psychotherapy practice. (For a fascinating contrary reading of similar events see Sigmund Freud's "The Uncanny" [1919] in SE 17). Is Jung pointing out simply that human beings will tend to see patterns when and where they *wish* to and hence find "meaningful" events which are in fact completely unrelated, except in their imaginations?

2. To illustrate a synchronistic event Jung describes a walk along the lake at the edge of which he finds a foot-long fish (p. 521). Why does he make a point of the fact that no one else was around? Why is it difficult for him to *avoid* the impression that such events are more than coincidental? Is it equally difficult for most people to avoid believing that they have special insight into extraordinary events which signify their relationship to extraordinary powers? When is one most likely to look for such "uncanny" events?

3. In his longer study Jung refers to his own attempt at correlating choice of marriage partner with astrological signs, as well as reports of J.B. Rhine's experiments with ESP, and similar efforts that aim at showing that (1) either a person's state of mind can influence objects at a distance, or (2) a person's character is influenced continually by stellar and planetary forces beyond his or her control. Are these, and similar ideas, logically coherent? That is, if one is true does it support necessarily the validity of the other? If not, why would we find them together so often, as in Jung's essay? (We read of a similar incident in MDR when Jung confronted Freud with claims of his paranormal powers.)

4. Returning to the issue of how character and expectation may affect psychic powers, Jung describes a female patient for whom a certain insect appeared "knocking against the window-pane" (p. 525). Why would this effect the cure he had aimed at in vain previously? That is, what must the young woman have believed about *Jung* when he produced, as it were out of thin air, the beetle? How would those beliefs have figured in her change of mood and self-understanding in that relationship?

5. Jung seems to fluctuate about the scientific character of astrology (pp. 528–531). What facts would, if discovered, cause him to identify it with the other sciences? Would he be entirely pleased by this alteration of its "mantic" character to a purely scientific one? Would persons who follow astrology in general be pleased or disappointed should physicists, for example, discover fixed and absolutely rational connections between personality types and the date of one's birth, or marriage, etc.?

6. Given Jung's feelings about astrology and ESP, how would he understand the process of therapy itself? That is, to what forces or agencies would he ascribe the responsibility for therapeutic progress? And how would most of his patients, in turn, experience him? In general, how would they come to look upon themselves *after* a successful treatment with Jung?

7. If Jung's explication of synchronicity is correct, the psyche cannot be localized entirely in ordinary space and time. How might religionists respond to this latter theorem? Which of their doctrines would resonate most closely with this understanding of the psyche? Many people seem to believe they are nothing other than corporeal entities, localized in space and time. Why are they wrong (if Jung is right)? How could one employ the concept of the collective unconscious *and* the theory of archetypes as organized sub-personalities to support Jung's claim?

8. In a famous section of his *Confessions* Saint Augustine describes how, in a moment of great despair over his conversion to Christianity, he heard, as if commanding him, voices chanting, "Take it up and read." He interpreted this to mean he should take up the New Testament texts and there read the first passage he happened upon. Why would he and countless others carry out such practices? Is it comparable to the casting of the *I Ching* (p. 527). (How might Freud explain Augustine's solution to his crisis?)

Aion: Researches into the Phenomenology of the Self (1951) CW 9.2

Technical Terms

Aion; ego; self; endosomatic perceptions; shadow; Maya; syzygy; anima and animus; shadow; Wise Old Man; Chthonic Mother; *marriage quaternio; daimon; coniunctio oppositorum; imago Dei*; individuation.

In this essay, of which we read the first seven chapters, Jung returns to the style and concerns he developed in *Symbols of Transformation*. Alongside technical passages on analytical theory and technique, we find extensive comments upon an immense variety of ancient texts that are unfamiliar to most readers. We cannot assess here the accuracy of Jung's scholarship; my goals are to elucidate his claims. Their verification is another, equally important matter.

1. Jung summarizes his theme in the foreword, pp. ix–xi. Why is it only natural that his reflections on the psychological meaning of Christ should center on the symbol of *Pisces*? The latter is a symbol found typically in pagan beliefs, notably astrology, with which the official Church has had little to do. In the same way most Christians would not find the statue of the Mithraic god, Aion (the frontispiece), compatible with their understanding of the meaning of Christ's mission on earth. Why are they wrong, at least psychologically? Why does Jung find the concomitant appearance of Jewish, Christian, Gnostic, and astrological ideas about the end of time a sure sign of their psychological validity? (See above our reading of his "On Synchronicity" [CW 8, pp. 520–531].)

2. In the first chapter Jung repeats some of the distinctions we have already come across. On what grounds, for example, does he distinguish the ego from the self, and both of these from the psyche? Of these three entities, which can vary most easily, for example through education, and which vary least? Given Jung's definition of the ego, why must we conclude that the "self" cannot be identified with consciousness (in the way it is usually)?

3. The "self" may confront the ego as an objective entity. Why can the ego not, in turn, eventually uncover the roots of the self and, through intensive analysis, "empty out" its contents? Why can the ego not perceive fully and exhaustively the nature of the substrate upon which the psyche rests?

4. In chapter two we learn that a person must "be convinced that he throws a very long shadow" (p. 9) before he or she is able to undo the projections cast upon the other. From our reading of Jung's dream theory and theory of interpretation can one amplify the likely rationale behind Jung's use of the term "shadow" to describe this archetype? For example, what determines the intensity, shape, and motility of a shadow in ordinary life? (Why would many naive conceptions of the soul or psyche refer to it as a "shadow"?)

5. The shadow is a moral problem (p. 8). What does the term moral mean in this context? Can analytic treatment help solve such moral questions? Does Jung allow that Freud's methods are pertinent to these kinds of problems? In the course of analytic treatment at what stage would one come across the shadow? Ought we to see its manifestations before or after the appearance of the persona? If the shadow is an archetype, and if religions are culturally devised systems for controlling the archetypes, what kind of

deities or spiritual beings must be included in any well-rounded pantheon?

6. Beyond the shadow lie the contra-sexual archetypes, the anima and animus. Again, assuming Jung's general understanding of the biological foundation of the psyche, why is a man's counter-soul always female, and a woman's always male? Why would confrontation with either be especially difficult in American culture? (Jung's language is purposefully mythological; for an illustration of the confrontation with the anima see chapter six in MDR.) How is the anima related to "My Lady Soul," Maya, and similar figures, like the Muses which Greek poets and their English devotees were wont to invoke?

7. When anima meets animus, the first "ejects her poison" and the second "draws his sword of power" (p. 15). Must the bickering and nonsense which Jung says typify such encounters persist in all relationships? In other words, how can the ego come to rely upon a well-functioning anima or animus? When this state occurs, how is each sex enhanced? (Why is it often easier to simply quote from these passages rather than explicate them; why is this so?)

8. The more civilized persons are, the more *unconscious* they are of their anima or animus (p. 21); hence, they are more prone to psychological disease, particularly neuroses. While the anima has been worshipped as a god, she no longer enjoys such respect except in the Catholic Church. Why has the latter institution always been personified as female? Why would Jung be especially fond of the astrological term "divine syzygy" when describing the Church's relationship to the Son? How does the union of the latter two entities constitute a divine marriage? Can ordinary mortals too participate in such a marriage? Why would Catholics have an advantage over non-Catholics? In other words, why are they more likely to comprehend the *marriage quaternio* (p. 22)?

9. When we turn to Jung's remarks on the self, we find what appear to be contradictions. It seems the self is both archetypal (related to the god-image) and aspects of one's conscious personality. Why is Jung so keen on Clement of Alexandria's remark about the knowledge of God and the knowledge of self. According to most Christian (and Jewish) authorities, can one know God, face to face, as one knows other, ordinary people? If not, in what does the knowledge of God's person consist? Is *this* what Jung means by knowledge of the self in its deepest sense?

10. We read, in "The Relations between the Ego and the Unconscious" (CW 7), already of the vicissitudes which marked the ego's attempts to approach and integrate the contents of the archetypes. Why are most such approaches disastrous? Yet, Jung says, some

people do find a way of approaching the archetypes, including the self, without succumbing to pathologies. How do they accomplish this? Indeed, why is their success a *moral* victory (p. 26)? Why does Jung prefer the Greek term *daimon* to the usual Christian sense of "God's will"?

11. "Value quanta" are easy to recognize, while collective ideals rarely have the same feeling tone (p. 29). What characterizes the former when they appear in an individual's experience (cf. the scale of values on p. 28)? But not all collective representations are as dry and affectless as the norm; Jung quotes from Hölderlin's poem to liberty (p. 29). Having read a great deal of Jung's thought on characteristics of poets and their psychological talents, what can we guess about Hölderlin himself? How and from what sources must he have derived his ability to reinform a shopworn cliche about liberty? Are his poems moral achievements?

12. We recall that Miss Miller began her fantasies on a vacation when she felt herself attracted to a handsome sailor. From there she elaborated the story of the Indian hero. Can we understand, in part, why her hero was a male? Miss Miller was later treated as a psychiatric patient. Was she mentally ill or was her culture inadequate to her needs? Why would persons like her, as well as religious mystics and poet-philosophers like Nietzsche, search for symbols which represent balance and harmony between opposites?

13. Jung seems anxious to avoid the appearance of merely deducing his psychological theorems. Why is he especially vulnerable to such accusations? That is, what aspects of the psyche's normal functioning tend toward unifying opposites in general, and why does this function, together with the factor of the unification of opposites, make Jung's system seem "preformed"?

14. At one point in time it seems most Europeans believed straightforwardly that there were numinous, personal powers, some evil and some good, which took a vital interest in one's everyday life and that certain religious actions would keep the former in check and force blessings from the latter. "What connection can there be between the world of such concepts and the everyday world, whose material reality is the concern of natural science . . ." (p. 35)? What is the end result of the rule of such sciences?

15. Christ is the culture hero of the West. Is this still true? If Jung's general psychological theory is valid, can modern Western people choose to avoid the dogmatic (churchly) assertions he elaborates in this chapter? Oddly enough Jung does not concern himself with the niceties of "scientific theology"; he emphasizes, rather, central dogmas, particularly those promulgated by the early Church and by its thinkers, like Augustine (pp. 38–40). What permits us to

return to such beliefs, which are surely contradicted by all the
scientific research carried out since the Enlightenment? Indeed,
how can Jung's psychology be a modern science if it reaffirms
consistently teachings which appear absolutely irrational and
incompatible with modern consciousness?

16. "There can be no doubt that the original Christian conception of
    the *imago Dei* embodied in Christ meant an all-embracing total-
    ity that even includes the animal side of man" (p. 41). Do most
    Sunday school teachers advance this theorem? If not, and if Jung
    is correct, what intervened between this original totalistic concep-
    tion of Christ, and the narrower portrait one finds in traditional,
    rationalized, teachings? Yet even Augustine failed to see what the
    Gnostics perceived directly. Why did the latter suffer punishment
    and eventual condemnation by the Church hierarchy? Why is
    Jung on their side?

17. The coming of the Antichrist is an inexorable law (p. 43). But has
    he come already, in some guise, to the West? Why did the verti-
    cality of the Gothic style give over to the "horizontal perspective"
    of the Renaissance (p. 43)? Although dogma tells us in Christ
    there is no east or west, He Himself is but one-half of the arche-
    type of the self. What or who is needed to make it complete? At
    the same time, why does Jung feel the Christian tradition itself
    can describe more accurately than any psychology the vicissitudes
    of the individual's coming to consciousness?

18. When one traces a condition back to "a psychic condition or fact,
    it is very definitely not reduced to nothing and thereby nullified"
    (p. 48). On what grounds does Jung employ this dictum to argue
    against Basil's theological opinion that evil is the privation of
    good? If no one can deny that evil is real, and perhaps as eternal
    as the good, why did the early Church fathers struggle to deny it
    anyway? Augustine, Aquinas, and the others were no fools: so
    why did they torture logic so cruelly?

19. Jung has a certain feeling for heretics and others whose thoughts
    led them to be condemned, if not obliterated, by the powers that
    be. For example, why is he fond of the so-called "Clement"
    (pp. 54–56) who described God's two hands, one that kills and the
    other that gives life? (We return to this theme, which fascinated
    Jung, below when we read *Answer to Job*.) How did the very
    earliest Christians rely upon their "greater unconsciousness"
    (p. 58) to save them from the errors of denying the reality and
    substantiality of evil? Indeed, how does that error account, per-
    haps, for the fact that it was Jewish Christians who elaborated the
    doctrine of God's two, antithetical sons?

20. "Since psychology is not metaphysics, no metaphysical dualisms

can be derived from . . . its statements" (p. 61). Why would his friend, Victor White, find Jung very close to the heretical Manichaeans? What psychological rationale does Jung offer in his defense against these charges? If the dualisms he finds throughout both religious and deep psychological thought are merely the result of our consciousness, which ascribes oppositional qualities to all it perceives, how can he employ them to predict future behaviors? We saw him accomplish this feat in his 1918 essay, "The Role of the Unconscious." He seems to accomplish similar feats with regard to the behavior of his patients.

21. This question in turn leads us back to the problem of the Antichrist and the reality of evil in history as well as the existence of an evil aspect of ourselves. How does Jung collapse these three issues in his representations of the dogmatic figure of Christ and the portrait of the psychological self (the archetypal self) in the two quaternio on p. 63? With these two portraits in mind, why does it follow that (1) Jesus was understood correctly as the *principium individuationis*, and (2) patients in analytical psychology draw spontaneously mandala figures as they recover from severe crises? (We see this most dramatically in MDR.)

22. The issue of veracity reappears when Jung says in a footnote, on p. 66, "Psyche is reality par excellence." If so, why does he not simply identify Christianity with the simple and ultimate truth and so tie himself completely to the Church? On the other side, if the Church has always known the essential truths which Jung has rediscovered in his clinic, why does it not identify itself completely with his teachings? The early Church employed the symbol of the fish; the alchemists sought the philosopher's stone in their common effort at representing the validity of their vision of Christ's essential nature. Both these symbols have little power in our time: what or who has replaced them? If there are *no* replacements and none are needed, can Jung's basic claims about Christ be accurate?

23. In non-Christian cultures we presume a common human biology and psychology give rise to a common set of archetypal constraints. Yet Taoism, Buddhism, and other major Eastern religions do not depend upon the Christ symbol. Can they offer, nevertheless, a valid road to salvation or spiritual resolution? Is being perfect in Christ equivalent to being a perfect person, or is it something else? Why must one take up the burden of wholeness if he or she wishes to avoid living in a world which appears fundamentally alien and conflictual? Is the wholeness Jung describes here equivalent to the concept mentioned in Third Force psychologies? (Jung was fascinated by the East and Eastern religion; see the index to the CW for more complete references to his many comments on both subjects.)

24. Jung returns to the question of Jesus' identification with the fish in chapter six. On what theoretical grounds can Jung contradict the usual explanation of Jesus' association with the fish? Do most contemporary churches explicate this and other theriomorphic aspects of Christ's nature? If not, and if Jung's historical reconstructions are sound, how can we explain the gap which separates the original Christian understanding of the creed as a "symbolum" (p. 73) from the watered-down version of our times?

25. On what additional grounds can Jung say, "But the sudden activation of the [fish] symbol" (p. 73) makes him suspect a second, major source for its association to Christ. There follows a long section which explicates ancient and medieval astrological speculations about the particular arrangements of the heavens which foretold the birth of Christ, and after his birth, the next great cataclysm, etc. (For explanations of the astrological signs Jung uses, see any good dictionary, e.g., the appendix to *Webster's New Collegiate Dictionary* [1975].)

26. Like alchemy, the other great medieval science with which Jung was fascinated, astrology is generally despised by contemporary thinkers. Is Jung arguing against the claims of modern scientists when he takes seriously these horoscopes of Christ? How does he explain, for example, the fact that in the year 7 B.C. there occurred three major conjunctions? How can astrological predictions that "were quite possible in antiquity" (p. 79) not be possible in our time?

27. Even readers friendly to Jung's phenomenological orientation may find it hard to understand sentences like, ". . . Joachim could have been seized by the archetype of the spirit. There is no doubt that his activities were founded on a numinous experience" (p. 85). Is this merely a way of speaking, or does Jung himself believe that Joachim and other visionaries foretold accurately our present conditions? If the former, why does Jung say we will be safer the more we know of the Antichrist? Why will the next swing of the pendulum, as symbolized by the aeon of Aquarius, be one in which evil is recognized in all its actual, ontological depth?

28. "Although no connection of any kind can be proved between the figure of Christ and the inception of the astrological age of the fishes" (p. 92), Jung does not abandon the idea of their union. Why not? What *psychological* principles, discovered independently of religious speculations, enable us to explain the surprising parallels we find between the astrological events and Christ's birth? Does Jung believe the Renaissance happened merely by chance? Or is our perception of the Renaissance, and its actors of themselves, conditioned by factors over which we have no control?

In the eight chapters which follow, Jung expands his investigation of fish symbolism and deepens his analysis of the mandala and quaternity symbols associated with Christ and the self. As interesting as those ideas are, we will turn to consider an equally remarkable text, *Answer to Job*. In it Jung reveals both the implications of his theory for rethinking the usual understanding of this text, and something of his own passion for religious understanding.

Answer to Job (1952) CW 11, *PJ* (519-650)

In this valuable work Jung sums up much of his general theory and states more clearly than before his own orientation toward religious issues. Chief among the latter is the problem of evil. What is its ontological status? Is it derived from God's will? In addition, why did Christianity divorce itself from its spiritual parent, Judaism? Is there an inherent developmental logic to the shape of Western religious history? As readers of MDR will recall, from early boyhood Jung felt keenly the sharpness of these questions; hence, Job appeared to him as something of a spiritual forefather with whose struggles and agony he identified himself deeply. The following questions follow roughly the twenty divisions of the CW text.

Technical Terms

Coincidentia Oppositorum; pleroma.

1. In his somber introduction Jung repeats his notion of phenomenological description (p. 360). He also defends the absolute validity of religious experiences against rationalist criticisms: *what* actual entities always underlie experiences of the divine? Why does he emphasize the degree to which archetypes impress one as if they possessed free will (p. 362)? Is this, in turn, tied to his inability to write about Job dispassionately? Does he in fact express himself fearlessly (p. 366)?

2. Unlike other commentators, Jung says Job's greatness lies in his theological beliefs: that Yahweh is both a unity and yet an antinomy (p. 369). Why would Jung find this so appealing and why celebrate what appears to be Yahweh's *distinct personality* and his irrational and distinctive response to Job? Indeed, why is God's fascination with Job, as an individual, a sure sign of the former's absolute *need* for the latter? How does Job's existence help establish and maintain Yahweh's?

3. Jung seems to argue that Yahweh was indeed a God superior to the other deities, particularly since he had no indecent past to live down. Yet why is his youth also a hindrance to him? Why, in analytical terms, does his own internal development require the

presence of *superior* human beings, like Job? What is the secret suspicion which Yahweh has about the very creatures he created out of dust and dirt? What is Job's sin (p. 378)?

4. Given Jung's description of Yahweh's immorality and his animal nature (p. 383), and given the developmental thesis of the entire book, what will characterize the dreams and visions of analytic patients as they confront for the first time the innermost archetypes? What gods will they also see? How does Jung account for the fact that most commentators do not perceive Yahweh's dual nature, nor perceive how highly Job is raised above him in moral value?

5. In part three, Jung discusses metaphysical speculations about Sophia (Wisdom) rampant during the time of the composition of the text of Job. What analytical principles does Jung draw upon to conclude that Yahweh's treatment of Job is an archaic projection of the God onto a blameless servant? Why did Yahweh himself need the aid of Sophia if he was to remain at Job's moral level? (Given this reading of Yahweh's character, ought we to find female divinities associated with Jesus in any full-fledged Christian metaphysics?) Must both Israel and the Church remain essentially female in theological conceptions? Why is the problem of evil a particularly masculine issue, while that of completion is particularly female (p. 395)?

6. In part four Jung advances well beyond the Old Testament text and suggests an inherent dynamism within Western spiritual development. How does he link Sophia, Eve, Lilith, and the Virgin Mary together in a grand description of the ineluctable development of an unconscious God to the New Testament visions of Jesus to the Assumption of Mary? Given this linkage is Jung, in part, saying that evil is an actual element of creation, not merely the absence of the good (*privatio boni*)?

7. One doubts that many devout Jews would agree with Jung's claims: why, according to the tenets of analytical psychology, would they be wrong? What tells us that, apart from any historical connection, Jesus and Mary are necessarily linked to the figures of Abel and Adam and Eve and Sophia? Why was the creation of humans in Yahweh's image a prefiguration of Christ? How did Sophia help "constellate" those psychic factors which gave rise to the appearance of Christ? On what grounds does Jung employ Egyptian mythology (p. 406) to supplement his explanation of the Old Testament prefigurations of Christ?

8. In part seven Jung analyzes aspects of Christ's character and asserts that on the Cross, Job's suffering was understood finally by the God who had up to that point remained partly unconscious. Is

this not pure Christian apologetics? How does Jung counter an argument that would reject his synthetic treatment of the Christ story and emphasize the mythical nature of Christ himself? What psychological factors would support Jung's contention that Christ represents a *symbolum* which is necessarily universal in its sources and importance?

9. Jung is especially concerned to elucidate the meaning of the sixth petition of the Lord's Prayer: why? What is the metaphysical implication of asking God to not lead one into evil (or to the Evil One)? How, in turn, does Jung link this element to the Catholic Church's teaching that revelation may continue, even after the period of canonization of the sacred texts (p. 413)? And why is Jung himself more convinced by the Catholics than by the Protestants who disavow Satan and the Holy Ghost?

10. The theme of the running together of opposites and the duality of God's nature return in part ten when Jung identifies the seventh petition of the Lord's Prayer, with Christ's prayer "My Father, if it be possible, let this cup pass from me" (p. 417). Why are both these petitions direct signs of the *heights* to which human beings have been lifted by Christ's sacrifice? Why is their appearance a measure of the degree to which Western spirituality has advanced beyond Job?

11. After championing the archetypal nature of Ezekiel's visions, which were written, perhaps, at the time of the composition of the book of Job, Jung notes that Gautama the Buddha lived at the same time in India. Given Jung's general theory of the archetypes and of synchronicity, how might one account for these nearly simultaneous events in world religion? How is each a "Son of Man" (p. 421)?

12. Jung then turns to the book of Enoch (pp. 421–429). Why are its date of composition (around 100 B.C.) and its fascination with quaternities sure signs of its place in the gradual maturation of the divine itself? Who or what "recalled" Sophia in this epoch (p. 423)? How, in fact, are Enoch's visions themselves both products of universal archetypes and "an answer to Job" (p. 427)? Jung sums up his view of Yahweh on p. 428: why is God's "instability" the inherent source of both creation and the divine drama of sin and redemption prefigured in Job, Ezekiel, and Enoch and made concrete in Christ's death?

13. What tells us that, given this divine drama, an enantiodromia "in the grand style" (p. 433) will entail necessarily the return of the evil or shadow side of God and a final confrontation between the forces of good and evil? When Jung speaks of the indwelling of the Holy Ghost and its effect on people like Saint Paul, is he

affirming Christian dogma or restating analytical principles? Why
has the Church failed to comprehend entirely the significance of
the Paraclete? How is this in turn related to the promulgation of
doctrines like *privatio boni*?

14. In examining the texts of the Epistles of John, Jung says their
    author was a bit too sure of himself and that therefore his visions
    actually contradicted his stated theological opinions. Many funda-
    mentalist preachers understand Revelation to record a prophetic
    vision: why does Jung feel John's Christ is a little too much like
    the unconscious of a "loving-Bishop"?

15. Although John's writings are full of hatred and vengeance, these
    non-Christian attributes are, Jung says, precisely what one would
    expect from someone whose consciousness is dominated by Christ.
    Why? Given Jung's developmental thesis, why would John's visions
    appear in response to Christ's teachings and the overwhelming mes-
    sage of love and forgiveness that suffuse the first three gospels?
    While Jung does not like John the man, why does he esteem John
    the prophet? Why is the latter the vehicle of the collective?

16. Jung lacerates the author of Revelation for his lack of Christian feel-
    ings, and notes how deeply unconscious are his themes. Why are
    they, in fact, indicators not of current but of future times? Why is
    the Book of Revelation properly placed at the end of the New Testa-
    ment? And how does its author exemplify Job's dilemma in his por-
    trait of God's dual nature? Does Jung doubt that synchronicity will
    fail to appear between the actual events in the West at the end of
    the second millennium and John's prophecies?

17. What is the universal religious nightmare to which Jung refers on
    p. 453? On what grounds and with what right does Jung put forth
    his descriptions of the source of a solution to this nightmare? Why
    cannot properly trained, academic theologians handle these
    issues? Why is it only in medical psychology, or perhaps the per-
    forming arts, that we find both the locus of suffering and a poten-
    tial source of renewal? Why does "God want to become man, but
    not quite" (p. 456)? Returning to the theme of evil as merely the
    absence of good, why does Jung link it to humans becoming over-
    weening and proud (and therefore evil)?

18. Is Jung's analysis of the effects of the Reformation (on pp. 457–458)
    a causal one? How has the Reformation contributed to our compara-
    tive blackness? If Jung's general line of argument is correct, can one
    say that revelations of divine intentions have ceased since the time
    when the official Church canon was established? How does Jung
    understand the Pope's then recent decision regarding the assump-
    tion of Mary to a celestial place (the *Assumptio Mariae*)?

19. It might appear that individuation is a process which one must seek

and struggle to achieve, as one struggles to achieve wealth and fame. Why is this a wrong understanding of this central process? How can it be that we may become unwitting victims of it and are "dragged along by fate" towards a goal we have not sought (p. 460)? Why does the theory of archetypes require us to see that no one may escape the demands of individuation any more than they can escape the demands of thirst and sexual longing?

20. In the same way, why are academic theologians remiss if they ignore the numerous stories, legends, and myths surrounding visions of Mary (or of UFO's) which occupy the minds of many ordinary people? What were the ultimate causes of the Pope's decision to declare Mary the Queen of Heaven? Although he was raised a Protestant, Jung seems to chide them; why have they failed to hear the yearnings of the consensus gentium? Jung died in the early 1960's. Would he be surprised by the upsurge in feminist theology since that time?

21. Yet is there a role for the "protests" which adhere to Protestantism itself? In the same way, if individuation occurs spontaneously and along genetically determined lines in all peoples at all times, why worry about it? Why can we not simply trust "Nature" to lead us along her natural lines? Why must we say both (1) the many gods are representations of the archetypes, and (2) the supreme and true god is represented only by the single archetype of the self?

22. In these final pages Jung returns to a theme we saw announced at the beginning of his work with the medium, SW: there are relatively autonomous factors or sub-personalities within each individual. For many other psychologists this describes either a psychotic personality or a hopelessly confused philosopher who refuses to assume responsibility for his entire life. How would Jung respond to both these criticisms? Why is he content to refer to Paul, who did not hestitate to claim divine sanction for his work, yet suffered all his life?

We consider this last question at length in the next chapter where we read *Memories, Dreams, Reflections*.

V

INDIVIDUATION AND SELF IN
MEMORIES, DREAMS, REFLECTIONS (1961)

Technical Terms

Rather than repeat the many terms discussed above, I refer readers to the excellent glossary at the end of MDR and to its index.

Considerations of the Text

I am reluctant to examine this book the way we have examined Jung's technical essays in the previous chapters. As the editor tells us, Jung stated explicitly he did not wish his autobiographical notes to be included within his *Collected Works*. While they have some of the tone and urgency of *Answer to Job*, these memoirs are much looser and less systematically developed than the arguments of that text. More so, having worked our way through many of Jung's major papers, we can read MDR easily and directly.

However, another reason for caution is that the book has a certain delicacy of argument which is easily overlooked if one treats it like a textbook. Critics of Jung might call it a certain vagueness and circularity. (For a vivid and sympathetic review by a famous Freudian psychoanalyst see D.W. Winnicott's "Review of C. Jung's *Memories, Dreams, Reflections*." *International Journal of Psycho-Analysis* [1964] 45, pp. 450–455.)

Yet MDR is a book too good to overlook and too illustrative of Jung's thinking for us not to consider it. I do so in the following. We examine the first eight chapters. (The last item in the appendix is still waiting for a definitive analysis, though some new ones have been offered.)

Prologue and Chapter I, First Years

1. For those who do not know Jung's life, his prologue might seem surprisingly devoid of references to other people. Why are others less important to him than the fiery magma of his inner experiencing? Are these dicta about the "other reality" incompatible

with the general theory we have seen him develop in the technical papers?

2. Why does it make sense to grant special relevance to a person's earliest memory? Consider the beginnings of other spiritual autobiographies: how do they initiate the reader into the personal myth? What characterizes these very early events: where are Jung's parents and family members? By what chain of associations does Jung connect his earliest memory to the corpse and from it to his father and then his mother?

3. His earliest memory of his mother is of her dress (p. 16). Why would he remember this *part* better than her face or voice or other individual characteristic?

4. Jung then describes a sequence of terrors and protective measures. What are the tone and quality of his terrors, and how might one connect his archetypal dream of the underground phallus with his previous anxieties? How do his feelings about Jesus and the "Man-eater" merge with his less articulated feelings about his mother and father? What is the "superior intelligence" (p. 14) at work in him? (When does the boy hurt himself? How are these episodes connected to his secret?)

5. Another remarkable story unfolds: the boy creates a secret representation of himself, the manikin and the manikin's stone. When does the boy feel compelled to examine it? Why does he hide it away from his family? Jung says that while the manikin was the crucial secret of his boyhood, he did not recall it until he was composing his *Symbols of Transformation* in 1910. How does he explain his sudden recollection? (See also below, chapter V.)

Chapter II, School Years

6. In this long chapter Jung describes a set of intense, emotional conflicts centered around a remarkable split in his personality into number one and a number two. Is the chapter as a whole elaborated around these two themes? For example, which of his personalities judges his parents and finds them wanting (pp. 24–25)?

7. He catalogues his social and scholastic troubles: which personality seems responsible for them? How does the boy understand his difficulties, and how does the theoretician explain them some seventy years later? How should we understand his severe neurotic sufferings (pp. 30–32)? What does the expression, "Now I am myself" mean (p. 32)? How does he connect this feeling with the feeling of security afforded him by remembering the manikin in the attic? (Do religious authorities offer similar assurances to true believers?)

8. Is the tale of Goethe (p. 35) truly annoying to the young boy? Does the old man telling us this story discount entirely the young boy's experiences of intense nostalgia for a past he could not have experienced? What was Jung's relationship to his father in the midst of these reveries about ancient times? And how do both sets of feelings reappear in the vision of God's destruction of the church? What is it that his father, the parson, had not understood?

9. "At such times I *knew* I was worthy of myself" (p. 45). What does this mean? When and with what previous feelings would one say this? What is it like to be *not* worthy of oneself? Why is the young boy embarrassed by his father's sermons? What does the older man overlook both in God's nature and in the very Bible upon which he preaches? Given our reading of the essay on Job, why does Jung say it would have opened his eyes had he read it?

10. Throughout the CW Jung refused to confess any religious beliefs. Is that true for these autobiographical notes too? In a similar vein, is Jung as skeptical here about matters of occult knowledge and the "inner eye" as he was in his technical papers? From whom does he trace these special gifts? Why is his father entirely inadequate and, compared to the mother, untouched by religious insights? For whom does one usually feel pity and from what vantage point (p. 55)?

11. Given the anxieties which the young boy suffers in school and at home, and given the nature of his visions and intuitions, and the massive split in himself, why is Jung not worried about his mental health? Why did he not object strenuously to the label "Father Abraham" (p. 66). Does he doubt that his No. 2 personality is inferior to Goethe's great characters, or even to the Biblical heroes? How does reading philosophy enable him to overcome previous neuroticisms? Yet, what threatens to throw him back into depression? How did his schoolmates' taunts inhibit his attempts to "overcome the inner split" (p. 72) in himself?

12. Under what circumstances is the split healed? Consider the accounts of the chemist (p. 76), his first inebriation (p. 77), the mountain (p. 77), and other moments in this chapter when he feels whole and unified: what characterizes these episodes? How does analytical theory account for Jung's vision of the alchemical apparatus (pp. 80–81)? And how might we account for the young man's passion for building fortifications. Why does this occur at the expense of his No. 2 personality?

Chapter III, Student Years

13. Since Jung wrote these memoirs late in his life there is every reason to feel confident in applying his general theory to their elucidation. For example, in this chapter he describes a sequence of personal crises: how should we understand the two dreams he has about this time (p. 85)? Are these full representations of individuation? If not, how can we account for both their archetypal qualities and their mandala features? *Faust* reappears: why at this time? Are there similar characters in American life and letters? If so, what are they? If not, is that a deficit?

14. Whence come dreams like his on p. 88? How does it portend his decision to assign the "I" to his No. 1 personality? We learn that his father was to have a major religious crisis: how does analytical theory permit him to account for his boyish visions and lifelong religious passions in the midst of such a spiritual malaise? Consider carefully Jung's feelings about his father in this chapter: how did Hamlet react to Claudius's prayers? Why is Jung outraged at *his* father's prayers (p. 93)?

15. Following his father's death and the latter's appearance in his dreams, Jung takes upon spiritualism with deep fascination: why? How do these readings, plus his medical training in morphology, and his passion for Nietzsche coincide in preparing him for his eventual choice of profession? How does he protect himself against Nietzsche's fate?

16. What emotional states precede the appearance of the unexplained events described on pp. 104–106? Why does Jung say it was his mother's No. 2 self which seemed to confirm his feeling that these were signs of some unnatural power? What was that power? How is each "synchronistic"? (Why preserve the pieces of the bread knife?) How does psychiatry enable him to find some healing and for the psyche to find a proper bed (p. 109)?

17. How, in general, do people respond to the death of family members? Does Jung exhibit any of these characteristics? What is the monastery of the world (p. 112)? Having read these descriptions of his subjective experiment, can one say Jung ever doubted God's existence? Did his phenomenological attitude obscure or enhance the force of his descriptions of religious artifacts?

Chapter IV, Psychiatric Activities

18. What were the woman's probable thoughts when she encouraged her children to drink the contaminated water? About so monstrous a crime Jung refused to inform the authorities or his colleagues. (Would Freud deny that in therapy the problem is

always the whole person, not merely the symptom alone?) Why is the old lady (pp. 118–119) his first *analysis*?

19. What gives Jung the courage (p. 126) to jump in and pester patients upon whom everyone else has given up? What tells him that paranoid ideas must have some meaning? (Had Freud denied this in his works of this period?) Does Jung advance a single form of therapy? Is shouting at the girl therapeutic? Would it work in all cases of early dementia? If there is no single method, what determines the therapist's style and technique in particular cases?

20. On what grounds does Jung inform the young woman (p. 139) that her problem is precisely her scoffing at her actual religious heritage? Does Jung believe in the possibility of second sight or other such paranormal capacities? Had he himself such skills? Why was her lack of "mythological ideas" (p. 139) a major impediment to her happiness? With what authority did Jung take upon himself the task of instilling in her the fear of God?

21. Does Jung like his patients? All of them? Why are intellectuals and habitual liars (p. 144) the most difficult to treat? Are the former among the optional neurotics who require mythical ideas and ideals for their happiness? Do his comments on his female patients match his theoretical comments on the anima figure?

We consider this question in more depth when we consider his description of his own psychotic-like confrontations with unconscious images and forces.

Chapter V, Sigmund Freud

22. Jung's comments on Freud have been much debated and discussed (see the appendix for works devoted to their analysis and for references to their letters as well as references in MDR). What is the tone of Jung's description of his meeting with the older man (pp. 149–151)?

23. What tells Jung that sexuality for Freud was a kind of *numinosum* (p. 150)? Given our reading of Jung's other essays on numinous experiences, with what, in analytical terms, is Freud preoccupied? If parapsychology is *not* a science (p. 151), who appears more correct—Jung and his acceptance of it, or Freud and his outright rejection? (Did Jung ever doubt the veracity of his visions or other paranormal events?)

24. If Jung is correct about Freud's characteristic denial of his own fascination with the occult, what kinds of behaviors and actions in later life should Freud have manifested around these themes? That is, if the rule of compensation operates as Jung says, how ought Freud to have responded to his own life crises? (For

relevant Freud texts see "The Uncanny," [(1919) SE 17]; "A Disturbance of Memory on the Acropolis" [(1936) SE 22] and "A Religious Experience" [(1928) SE 21].)

25. After reporting the catalytic exteriorization phenomenon (p. 155) Jung says Freud stared at him, aghast: can we surmise what Freud was thinking? At what point in their conversation and relationship did Jung first feel this phenomenon coming on? Are there any reasons why Freud might feel the younger man was indeed harboring very strong feelings toward him? (What kind of power would underlie one's capacity to transmit the force of one's red-hot diaphragm across a room?)

26. Jung's description of both Freud and himself has become a point of much discussion in the literature on both men. As he says, it has fed the argument on both sides of the "war" (p. 160). Of distinct interest are his dream and his claim that it gave him an inkling of the collective: how? Why would a dream give such a precise and detailed image of the actual structure of the psyche? Could Freud have agreed that dreams have no legerdemain?

27. How does Jung describe himself and his conscious wishes vis-à-vis the dream of the customs official and its wishes or intentions? On what grounds does he distinguish between the first half, where Freud is portrayed as a peevish old man, and the second, which portrays a heroic knight? Who is the latter? Reflecting back to the manikin in the little box, how might one understand Jung's very strong feeling for the Grail Legend (and alchemy, as well)? Against whom and with what authority did the knights of the Middle Ages struggle? (How were Jews portrayed in this period?)

28. Is incest a complication in only the rarest of cases? Did Jung's patient (on pp. 128–129), who had been sexually seduced by her brother, first develop the notion of incest as a royal prerogative, and then develop symptoms, or did the symptoms precede the royal-couple fantasy? In the same way, what findings in anthropology or the history of religion might help us decide between Jung's claims that sexuality is primarily "spiritual" (or "intellectual" in the sense of the German term *Geist*) and Freud's? Would the analysis of temporal sequences help us favor one side over another?

Chapter VI, Confrontation with the Unconscious

29. In this crucial chapter Jung describes the severe psychological trials he underwent following his break with Freud. Are these trials similar to those Miss Miller suffered as well? Why does it make sense that Jung's dream (on p. 171) occurs around Christmas? To what other elements in his life are these dream events

connected, especially the knight from the twelfth century? How should we explain his happening upon the pyramidal stone (p. 174) and the recovery of his underground phallus dream?

30. Jung never claims his ideas are new: in fact he argues precisely the opposite. Yet they are new to our century. Why was it given to someone like him to re-discover these concepts (or truths), while others, equally gifted and even more brilliant, like Nietzsche, fell into psychological illness? How did Jung preserve himself against their fate?

31. Does Jung assume full responsibility for his visions? If not, on what grounds does he distinguish what is merely his and what collective? How does he distinguish his dreams from his conscious fantasies? And who is Siegfried (pp. 179–180), whom he must slay yet whom he loves? In the midst of elaborating these fantasies, and painting his dreams, he finds a dead kingfisher (p. 183). Why does this strike him so hard? What ideas must finding it have aroused in him?

32. "I was like a patient in analysis with a ghost and a woman" (p. 186). How do both serve his task of expressing these banal or vulgar images and of preserving himself against utter destruction? How, in turn, does personifying these formerly unconscious "personalities" strip them of their power (p. 187)? How, again, did Jung avoid suffering the fate of his patients who reported and experienced similar fantasies to their detriment?

33. "These conversations with the dead formed a kind of prelude to what I had to communicate to the world" (p. 192). The only way to test out this remarkable statement is to examine carefully the text of the *Septem Sermones ad Mortuos* in the appendix to MDR. Are Jung's comments in this chapter the products of true belief or more phenomenology? Does it make any difference, finally, if such autonomous fantasies come from the outer or the inner world? Does Jung doubt that something real and powerful produced actual effects both in himself and in his family?

34. The dream he describes on pp. 197–198 is a particularly vivid portrait of both his feelings about his own life's work and exemplifies what he means by the terms mandala and individuation. Does Jung feel his are entirely new discoveries, brought about by the advance of scientific technique? If so, what weight and authority does he grant to traditional forms of peer review, experimentation, and other types of critical and public examination of one's hypotheses and claims? Another way of asking this is: what status does he grant the ego, and where does he delimit its authority over other parts of the psyche?

Chapter VII, The Work

35. Do most contemporary psychologists believe that their work depends upon a deep and sympathetic knowledge of history, particularly of arcana like European and Chinese alchemy? Why was Jung so pleased to find that analytical psychology was not a new science; that, indeed, it represented the re-emergence of ancient, and often despised, ideas? (Does Jung here treat the legend of his relationship to Goethe as an annoying bit of family presumptuousness?)

36. "...[T]he *coniunctio* was accompanied or heralded by dreams" (p. 213). Why does Jung put this forth as a positive claim? Could one not argue that his dreams were responses to and confirmations of his personal wishes, rather than guides and heralds? From which theorems of his dream theory would Jung have to draw his answer to this critique? (What is it about the phenomenology of dreams which lends to them such authority in his eyes?)

37. Regarding the composition of both *Aion* and *Answer to Job* (discussed above), Jung says he felt bound to consider the dark side of God's nature, though he resisted the task for many years (p. 216). What elements in his boyhood foreshadowed these questions and his resistance to them? Why does he not touch his head down completely (p. 219)? Jung links his resistance to his later reflections on Job's greatness: is the latter entirely unlike that of God? Could any single theological system of strict beliefs satisfy Jung's quest and questions?

Chapter VIII, The Tower

38. In these evocative descriptions of his private place, one finds very little of technical interest, but a great deal of biographical value. For example, why does Jung say it was only in the tower that his No. 2 personality could achieve a rightful hearing? In what other periods of his life have we seen him feel so strongly about physical objects? (Although it appears a staple of many nature-lovers, why does Jung feel that chopping wood, and so forth, is *simpler* than turning up the thermostat?)

39. Returning to the question of Jung and ordinary Christian faith we note his comments on Merlin (p. 228). Why would so many find it difficult to understand (or accept) the dark figure of Lucifer-Mercurius-Merlin? In light of Jung's own story, how many people would have his capacities and ability to confront the unconscious as he did? Given that many do not, and that Jung himself is surprised by this fact again and again, what alternative is available to the many who cannot understand? Are traditional religions an adequate answer—in Jung's estimation?

40. To what extent is analytical psychology nothing more than Jung's own, richly elaborated, myth? If it is predominately his story, as his grandparents and children are his and not ours, how much weight can we place upon his general conclusions? In other words, on what grounds does Jung claim his insights, dreams, visions and intuitions are more than fascinating products of an individual psyche? Even if one accepts his claims of clairvoyance and such, what value can they bear for us who may be far less talented?

41. Most of us do not have Jung's talents, nor share his particular fascination with the occult and arcane subjects like alchemy and gnosticism. Does this mean that, ultimately, his life and thought are irrelevant to us? Is happiness, in part, as he says, a matter of coming to terms with one's historical family? Can we too live in many centuries simultaneously?

APPENDIX

I Texts and Reference Works

The standard scholarly edition of Jung's translated works is the *Collected Works of C. G. Jung*, translated by R. F. C. Hull and others, printed in 20 volumes by Princeton University Press for the Bollingen Foundation. Each volume contains a complete listing of the contents of the entire set. Princeton has also published many CW volumes in paperback, see Books in Print. For abstracts of the CW see *Abstracts of the Collected Works of C. G. Jung*. Ed. C. L. Rothgeb, et al., Rockville, MD. National Institute of Mental Health, 1978.

Other text resources are: *The Portable Jung*, edited by Joseph Campbell (New York: Viking Press, 1971). It is an invaluable paperback collection of major papers the whole of which are described in Campbell's lengthy introductory essay.

In addition to these is Jung's autobiography, *Memories, Dreams, Reflections* (New York: Random, 1962), which he refused to include in the CW. It is a vivid and provocative account of his inner life and by far the best illustration of the crucial concept of individuation. It is available in paperback, has excellent appendixes, and a glossary of major Jungian terms.

II Bibliographies

The only major bibliography in English I am aware of is: *C. G. Jung and Analytical Psychology: A Comprehensive Bibliography*, by Joseph F. Vincie (New York: Garland Publishing, 1977). Its 297 pages describe nearly four thousand books and articles, arranged in chronological order, with excellent subject and author indices. It lists book reviews of Jung's works and it describes journals relevant to Jung and analytical psychology. Its LC number is Z8458.75.v55 [BF173.J85].

Additional bibliographies are available in: Mattoon, Mary Ann, *Jungian Psychology in Perspective*. New York: Free Press; London: Collier Macmillan, 1981, 334 pp.

Letters, Manuscripts, and Collected Papers

In addition to the CW indices and bibliographies on Jung's writings, see Vincent Brome, *Jung* (New York: Atheneum, 1978), pp. 314ff: "Other Sources."

For a review of journal articles in addition to Vincie, see pp. 119ff in Corsini, Raymond J., ed., *Current Personality Theories*. Itasca, Ill.: F.E. Peacock Publishers, 1977, 465 pp.

For original works on alchemy see also, *Alchemy and the Occult: A Catalogue of Books and Manuscripts from the Collection of Paul and Mary Mellon Given to Yale University Library*, compiled by Ian McPhail. New Haven: Yale University Press, 1968–77, 4 vols.

See also *Catalogue of the Kristine Mann Library of the Analytical Psychology Club of New York, Inc.*. Boston: G. K. Hall, 1978.

III Journals

Anima
Analytical Psychology Club of Los Angeles
Analytical Psychology Club of New York
C. G. Jung Institute of San Francisco
C. G. Jung Institute, Zurich
Guild of Pastoral Psychology
Harvest
Inward Light
Journal of Analytical Psychology
Papers of the Analytical Psychology Club of New York
Papers from the Eranos Yearbooks
Psychological Perspectives
Quadrant
San Francisco Jung Institute Library Journal
Spring

For a list of foreign language journals, including the Swiss journals, see pp. xi–xii in Vincie, *Comprehensive Bibliography*, above.

For an excellent review of the Eranos Yearbook volumes, from 1933 to 1976, see Donna J. Scott and Charles E. Scott, "Eranos and Eranos *Jahrbucher*," *Religious Studies Review*, 8:3 (1982), pp. 226–239. They describe the series as a whole and summarize the content of the first forty-five volumes.

IV History of Analytical Psychology

Alexander, Franz Gabriel, *Psychoanalytic Pioneers*, ed. Franz Alexander, Samuel Eisenstein, and Martin Grotjahn. New York: Basic Books, 1966, 616 pp.

Ellenberger, Henri F., *The Discovery of the Unconscious: The History and Evolution of Dynamic Psychiatry*. New York: Basic Books, 1970, 932 pp.

Evans, Richard Isadore, *Conversations with Carl Jung and Reactions from Ernest Jones*. Van Nostrand Reinhold Co., 1964, 173 pp.

Hogenson, George B., *Jung's Struggle with Freud*. Notre Dame: University of Notre Dame Press, 1983, 160 pp.

Homans, Peter, *Jung in Context: Modernity and the Making of a Psychology*. Chicago: University of Chicago Press, 1979, 234 pp.

Hoop, Johannes Hermanus van der, *Nieuwe richtingen in de zielkunde*; English, *Character and the Unconscious: A Critical Exposition of the Psychology of Freud and of Jung*. Authorized translation by Elizabeth Trevelyan. College Park, Md.: McGrath Publishing Co., 1970, 222 pp.

Kaufmann, Walter Arnold, *Freud versus Adler and Jung*. New York: McGraw-Hill, 1980, 494 pp.

Rieff, Philip, *The Triumph of the Therapeutic: Uses of Faith after Freud*. 1st ed. New York: Harper and Row, 1966, 274 pp.

Roazen, Paul, *Freud and His Followers*. 1st ed. New York: Knopf, 1975, 602 pp.

Steele, Robert S., *Freud and Jung: Conflicts of Interpretation*. Boston: Routledge & Kegan Paul, 1982, 390 pp.

Thompson, Clara Mabel, *Psychoanalysis: Evolution and Development*. London: Allen and Unwin, 1952, 252 pp.

Wyss, Dieter, *Depth Psychology: A Critical History, Development, Problems, Crises*. Trans. Gerald Onn. New York: W.W. Norton, 1966, 568 pp.

V General Works and Introductions to Jung

Arieti, Silvano, editor-in-chief, *American Handbook of Psychiatry*. 6 vols. 2nd ed. New York: Basic Books, 1974-75.

Barton, Anthony, *Three Worlds of Therapy: An Existential-Phenomenological Study of the Therapies of Freud, Jung, and Rogers*. 1st ed. Palo Alto, Ca.: Mayfield Publishing Co., 1974, 271 pp.

Bennet, Edward Armstrong, *C.G. Jung*. New York: Dutton, 1962/61.

Bennet, Edward Armstrong, *What Jung Really Said*. New York: Schocken Books, 1966/67, 186 pp.

Brome, Vincent, *Jung*. 1st American ed. New York: Atheneum, 1978, 327 pp.

Carotenuto, Aldo, *Diario di una Segreta Simmetria*. English: *A Secret Symmetry: Sabrina Spielrein between Jung and Freud*. Trans. Arno Pomerans, John Shepley, Krishna Winston. 1st American ed. New York: Pantheon Books, 1982, 250 pp.

Clark, Robert Alfred, *Six Talks on Jung's Psychology*. Pittsburgh: Boxwood Press, 1953, 84 pp.

Cohen, Edmund D., *C.G. Jung and the Scientific Attitude*. New York: Philosophical Library, 1974, 167 pp.

Corrie, Joan, *ABC of Jung's Psychology*. London: Kegan Paul, Trench Trubner & Co., Ltd., 1927, 96 pp.

Corsini, Raymond J., ed., *Current Personality Theories*. Itasca, Ill.: F.E. Peacock Publishers, 1977, 465 pp.

Corsini, Raymond J., ed., *Current Psychotherapies*. Itasca, Ill.: F.E. Peacock Publishers, 1973, 502 pp.

Dry, Avis M., *The Psychology of Jung: A Critical Interpretation*. London: Methuen; New York: Wiley, 1961, 329 pp.

Evans, Richard Isadore, *Jung on Elementary Psychology: A Discussion between C.G. Jung and Richard I. Evans*. 1st ed. New York: Dutton, 1976, 242 pp.

Fodor, Nandor, *Freud, Jung, and Occultism*. New Hyde Park, N.Y.: University Books, 1971, 272 pp.

Fordham, Frieda, *An Introduction to Jung's Psychology*. 3rd ed. New York: Penguin Books, 1966, 158 pp.

Fordham, Michael Scott Montague ed., *Contact with Jung: Essays on the Influence of his Work and Personality*. Philadelphia: Lippincott, 1963, 245 pp.

Franz, Marie-Louise von, *C.G. Jung: His Myth in Our Time*. Trans. William H. Kennedy. New York: Putnam, 1975, 355 pp.

Frey-Rohn, Liliane, *Von Freud zu Jung*. English: *From Freud to Jung: A Comparative Study of the Psychology of the Unconscious*. Trans. Fred E. Engreen and Evelyn K. Engreen. New York: Putnam, 1974, 345 pp.

Glover, Edward, *Freud or Jung?* London: Allen and Unwin, 1950, 207 pp.

Hall, Calvin Springer, *A Primer of Jungian Psychology*. New York: Taplinger Publishing Co., 1973, 142 pp.

Hall, Calvin Springer, *Theories of Personality*. 2nd ed. New York: Wiley, 1970, 622 pp.

Hannah, Barbara, *Jung, His Life and Work: A Biographical Memoir*. New York: Perigee Books, 1981, 376 pp.

Jacobi, Jolande Szbekbacs, *The Psychology of C.G. Jung*. Trans. Ralph Manheim. 8th ed. New Haven/London: Yale University Press, 1973, 203 pp.

Jaffe, Aniela, ed., *C.G. Jung, Bild und Wort*. English: *C.G. Jung, Word and Image*. Princeton, N.J.: Princeton University Press, 1979, 238 pp.

Jaffe, Aniela, *Aus Leben und Werkstatt von C.G. Jung*. English: *From the Life and Work of C.G. Jung*. Trans. R.F.C. Hull. New York: Harper and Row, 1971, 137 pp.

Jaffe, Aniela, *Der Mythus vom Sinn im Werk von C.G. Jung*. English: *The Myth of Meaning in the Work of C.G. Jung*. Trans. R.F.C. Hull. London: Hodder and Stoughton, 1970, 186 pp.

Jung, Carl G., *Man and His Symbols*. Garden City, N.Y.: Doubleday, 1964, 320 pp.

Maddi, Salvatore R., *Personality Theories: A Comparative Analysis*. 4th ed. Homewood, Ill.: Dorsey Press, 1980, 772 pp.

Mattoon, Mary Ann, *Jungian Psychology in Perspective*. New York: Free Press; London: Collier Macmillan, 1981, 334 pp.

Meier, Carl Alfred, *Jung and Analytical Psychology*. Newton Centre, Mass.: Department of Psychology, Andover Newton Theological School, 1959, 80 pp.

Meier, Carl Alfred, *The Psychology of C. G. Jung*, Vol. I. Trans. Eugene Rolfe. Santa Monica, Ca.: Sigo Press, 1982, 256 pp.

Progoff, Ira, *Depth Psychology and Modern Man: A New View of the Magnitude of Human Personality, Its Dimensions and Resources*. New York: McGraw-Hill, 1959, 277 pp.

Progoff, Ira, *Jung's Psychology and Its Social Meaning*. Garden City, N.Y.: Anchor Press/Doubleday, 1953, 290 pp.

Progoff, Ira, *The Symbolic and the Real: A New Psychological Approach to the Fuller Experience of Personal Existence*. New York: McGraw-Hill, 1963, 234 pp.

Stern, Paul J., *C.G. Jung—The Haunted Prophet*. New York: G. Braziller, 1976, 267 pp.

Storr, Anthony, *C.G. Jung*. New York: Viking Press, 1973, 116 pp.

Van der Post, Laurens, *Jung and the Story of Our Time*. 1st ed. New York: Pantheon Books, 1975, 276 pp.

Wehr, Gerhard, *C.G. Jung in Selbstzeugnissen und Bilddokumenten*. English: *Portrait of Jung: An Illustrated Biography*. Trans. W. Hargreaves. New York: Herder and Herder, 1971, 173 pp.

Winski, Norman, *Understanding Jung*. Los Angeles: Sherbourne Press, 1971, 140 pp.

Wolman, Benjamin B., ed., *Handbook of Child Psychoanalysis: Research, Theory, and Practice*. New York: Van Nostrand Reinhold Co., 1972, 643 pp.

Wolman, Benjamin B., ed., *Psychoanalytic Techniques: A Handbook for the Practicing Psychoanalyst*. New York: Basic Books, 1967, 596 pp.

VI Essays on Therapeutic Technique

Fordham, Michael Scott Montague, *Jungian Psychotherapy: A Study in Analytical Psychology*. Chichester, England/New York: Wiley, 1978, 185 pp.

Fordham, Michael Scott Montague, *New Developments in Analytical Psychology*. London: Routledge and Kegan Paul, 1957, 214 pp.

Fordham, Michael Scott Montague, *The Objective Psyche*. London: Routledge and Kegan Paul, 1958, 214 pp.

Fordham, Michael, ed., *Technique in Jungian Analysis*. London: Heinemann Medical, 1974, 335 pp.

Franz, Marie-Louise von, *Spiegelungen der Seele*. English: *Projection and Re-Collection in Jungian Psychology: Reflections of the Soul*. Trans. William H. Kennedy. La Salle, Ill.: Open Court, 1980, 253 pp.

Franz, Marie-Louise von, "The Inferior Function" with James Hillman, "The Feeling Function" in *Lectures on Jung's Typology*. Irving, Texas: Spring Publications, 1979, 150 pp.

Greene, Liz, *Relating: An Astrological Guide to Living with Others on a Small Planet*. 2nd ed. New York: S. Weiser, 1978, 294 pp.

Guggenbuhl-Craig, Adolf, *Marriage: Dead or Alive*. Trans. Murray Stein. Zurich: Spring Publications, 1977, 126 pp.

Guggenbuhl-Craig, Adolf, *Macht als Gefahr beim Helfer*. English: *Power in the Helping Professions*. New York: Spring Publications, 1971, 155 pp.

Hall, James Albert, *Clinical Uses of Dreams: Jungian Interpretations and Enactment*. New York: Grune and Stratton, 1977, 367 pp.

Hannah, Barbara, *Encounters with the Soul: Active Imagination as Developed by C.G. Jung*. Santa Monica, CA: Sigo Press, 1981, 254 pp.

Harding, Mary Esther, *The "I" and the "Not-I": A Study in the Development of Consciousness*. Princeton, N.J.: Princeton University Press, 1973, 244 pp.

Harding, Mary Esther, *The Parental Image: Its Injury and Reconstruction: A Study in Analytical Psychology*. New York: Putnam, 1965, 238 pp.

Hillman, James, *The Dream and the Underworld*. 1st ed. New York: Harper and Row, 1979, 243 pp.

Hillman, James, *Inter Views: Conversations on Psychotherapy*. New York: Harper & Row, 1982, n.p.

Hillman, James, *Loose Ends: Primary Papers in Archetypal Psychology*. Zurich: Spring Publications, 1975, 212 pp.

Hillman, James, *The Myth of Analysis: Three Essays in Archetypal Psychology*. New York: Harper Colophon, 1978, 313 pp.

Hillman, James, *Suicide and the Soul*. Irving, Texas: Spring Publications, 1976, 191 pp.

Hinkle, Beatrice (Moses), *The Re-Creating of the Individual: A Study of Psychological Types and Their Relation to Psychoanalysis.* New York: Dodd, Mead, 1949, 465 pp.

Hochheimer, Wolfgang, *Die Psychotherapie von C.G. Jung.* English: *The Psychotherapy of C.G. Jung.* Trans. Hildegard Nagel. New York: Putnam, 1969, 160 pp.

Hoop, Johannes Hermanus van der, *Conscious Orientation: A Study of Personality Types in Relation to Neurosis and Psychosis.* Trans. Laura Hutton. New York: Harcourt, Brace, 1937, 352 pp.

Jaffe, Aniela, *Apparitions and Precognition: A Study from the Point of View of C.G. Jung's Analytical Psychology.* New Hyde Park, N.Y.: University Books, 1963, 214 pp.

Kalff, Dora M., *Sandplay: Mirror of a Child's Psyche.* San Francisco: Browser Press, 1971, 175 pp.

Kalff, Dora M., *Sandspiel.* English: *Sandplay: A Psychotherapeutic Approach to the Psyche.* Santa Monica, Ca.: Sigo Press, 1980, 169 pp.

Keirsey, David, *Please Understand Me: An Essay on Temperament Styles.* 3rd ed. Del Mar, Ca.: Promethean Nemesis Books, 1978, 210 pp.

Lawrence, Gordon, *People Types and Tiger Stripes: A Practical Guide to Learning Styles.* Gainesville, Florida: Center for Applications of Psychological Type, 1979, n.p.

Lowen, Walter, *Dichotomies of the Mind: A Systems Science Model of the Mind and Personality.* New York: Wiley, 1982, 314 pp.

Mahoney, Maria F., *The Meaning in Dreams and Dreaming: The Jungian Viewpoint.* Secaucus, N.J.: Castle Books, 1966, 256 pp.

Mattoon, Mary Ann, *Applied Dream Analysis: A Jungian Approach.* Washington: V.H. Winston; New York: Halsted Press, 1978, 253 pp.

McCully, Robert S., *Rorschach Theory and Symbolism: A Jungian Approach to Clinical Material.* Baltimore: Williams and Wilkins, 1971, 271 pp.

Meier, Carl Alfred, *Ancient Incubation and Modern Psychotherapy.* Trans. Monica Curtis. Evanston, Ill.: Northwestern University Press, 1967, 152 pp.

Moustakas, Clark E., ed., *The Self: Explorations in Personal Growth.* New York: Harper and Row, 1956, 284 pp.

Rossi, Ernest Lawrence, *Dreams and the Growth of Personality: Expanding Awareness in Psychotherapy.* New York: Pergamon Press, 1972, 217 pp.

Sanford, John A., *Between People: Communicating One-to-One.* New York: Paulist Press, 1982, 92 pp.

Sanford, John A., *Dreams and Healing*. New York: Paulist Press, 1978, 164 pp.

Sanford, John A., *Dreams: God's Forgotten Language*. Philadelphia: Lippincott, 1968, 223 pp.

Sanford, John A., *Evil: The Shadow Side of Reality*. New York: Crossroad, 1981, 161 pp.

Sanford, John A., *Healing and Wholeness*. New York: Paulist Press, 1977, 162 pp.

Sanford, John A., *The Kingdom Within: A Study of the Inner Meaning of Jesus' Sayings*. 1st ed. Philadelphia: Lippincott, 1970, 226 pp.

Sanford, John A., *Ministry Burnout*. New York: Paulist Press, 1982, 117 pp.

Shapiro, Kenneth Joel and Irving E. Alexander, *The Experience of Introversion: An Integration of Phenomenological, Empirical, and Jungian Approaches*. Durham, N.C.: Duke University Press, 1975, 180 pp.

Singer, June K., *Boundaries of the Soul: The Practice of Jung's Psychology*. 1st ed. Garden City, N.Y.: Doubleday, 1972, 420 pp.

Stein, Robert, *Incest and Human Love: The Betrayal of the Soul in Psychotherapy*. Baltimore: Penguin Books, 1973, 200 pp.

Wheelwright, Joseph B., ed., *The Analytic Process: Aims, Analysis, Training*. New York: Putnam for the C.G. Jung Foundation of Analytical Psychology, 1971, 316 pp.

Whitmont, Edward C., *Psyche and Substance: Essays on Homeopathy in the Light of Jungian Psychology*. Richmond, CA: North Atlantic Books, 1980, 190 pp.

Williams, Strephon Kaplan, *Jungian-Senoi Dreamwork Manual*. New ed. Berkeley, CA: Journey Press, 1980, 300 pp.

Woodman, Marion, *The Owl Was a Baker's Daughter: Obesity, Anorexia Nervosa and the Repressed Feminine: A Psychological Study*. Toronto: Inner City Books, 1980, 139 pp.

VII Essays on Theory

Adler, Gerhard, ed., *Current Trends in Analytical Psychology*. London: Tavistock, 1961, 326 pp.

Adler, Gerhard, Edward C. Whitmont, and Erich Neumann, *Dynamic Aspects of the Psyche*. New York: Analytical Psychology Club of New York, 1956, 72 pp.

Adler, Gerhard, *Dynamics of the Self*. London: Coventure, 1979, 177 pp.

Adler, Gerhard, *The Living Symbol: A Case Study in the Process of Individuation*. New York: Pantheon Books, 1961, 463 pp.

Adler, Gerhard, *Studies in Analytical Psychology*. New York: Putnam for the C.G. Jung Foundation for Analytical Psychology, 1966, 250 pp.

Adler, Gerhard, ed., *Success and Failure in Analysis*. New York: Putnam for the C.G. Jung Foundation for Analytical Psychology, 1974, 231 pp.

Barker, Culver Maynard, *Healing in Depth*. Ed. H.I. Bach. London: Hodder and Stoughton, 1972, 191 pp.

Baynes, Helton Godwin, *Mythology of the Soul: A Research into the Unconscious from Schizophrenic Dreams and Drawings*. New ed. London: Rider, 1969, 980 pp.

Berry, Patricia, ed., *Fathers and Mothers: Five Papers on the Archetypal Background of Family Psychology*. Zurich: Spring Publications, 1973, 141 pp.

Bertine, Eleanor, *Jung's Contribution to Our Time: The Collected Papers of Eleanor Bertine*. Ed. Elizabeth C. Rohrbach. New York: Putnam for the C.G. Jung Foundation for Analytical Psychology, 1967, 271 pp.

Bolen, Jean Shinoda, *The Tao of Psychology: Synchronicity and the Self*. 1st ed. San Francisco: Harper and Row, 1979, 111 pp.

Christou, Evangelos, *The Logos of the Soul*. Vienna/Zurich: Dunquin Press, 1963, 104 pp.

Crookall, Robert, *The Jung-Jaffe View of Out-of-the-body Experiences*. London: World Fellowship for the Churches' Fellowship for Psychical and Spiritual Studies, 1970, 134 pp.

Davis, Robert Wm., ed., *Toward a Discovery of the Person*. Burbank, CA: Society for Personality Assessment, 1974, 83 pp.

Edinger, Edward F., *Ego and Archetype: Individuation and the Religious Function of the Psyche*. New York: Putnam for the C.G. Jung Foundation for Analytical Psychology, 1972, 304 pp.

Fordham, Michael Scott Montague, *Children as Individuals*. 1st American ed. New York: Putnam for the C.G. Jung Foundation for Analytical Psychology, 1969, 223 pp.

Fordham, Michael Scott Montague, *New Developments in Analytical Psychology*. London: Routledge and Kegan Paul, 1957, 214 pp.

Fordham, Michael Scott Montague, *The Self and Autism*. London: Heinemann Medical [for] the Society of Analytical Psychology, 1976, 296 pp.

Franz, Marie-Louise von, *On Divination and Synchronicity: The Psychology of Meaningful Chance*. Toronto: Inner City Books, 1980, 123 pp.

Franz, Marie-Louise von, *Time: Rhythm and Repose*. New York: Thames and Hudson, 1978, 96 pp.

Franz, Marie-Louise von, *Zahl und Zeit*. English: *Number and Time: Reflections Leading toward a Unification of Depth Psychology and Physics*. Trans. Andrea Dykes. Evanston, Ill.: Northwestern University Press, 1974, 332 pp.

Frey-Wehrlin, C.T., ed., *Festschrift zum 60*. Geburtstag C.A. Meier, hrsg. von C.T. Frey-Wehrlin. Zurich: Rascher, 1965, 277 pp.

Guggenbuhl-Craig, Adolf, ed., *Der Archetyp: The Archetype*. Basel, New York: Krager, 1964, 234 pp.

Guggenbuhl-Craig, Adolf, *Seelenwhusten*. English: *Eros on Crutches: Reflections on Psychopathy and Amorality*. Trans. Gary V. Hartman. Irving, Texas: Spring Publications, 1980, 126 pp.

Harding, Mary Esther, *Psychic Energy: Its Source and Goal*. New York: Pantheon Books, 1947, 497 pp.

Harding, Mary Esther, *Psychic Energy: Its Source and Its Transformation*. Princeton, N.J.: Princeton University Press, 1973, 497 pp.

Head, Rhoda, Rose-Emily Rothenberg, and David Wesley, eds., *A Well of Living Waters: A Festschrift for Hilde Kirsch*. Los Angeles: C.G. Jung Institute, 1977, 282 pp.

Hillman, James, *Emotion: A Comprehensive Phenomenology of Theories and Their Meanings for Therapy*. 2nd ed. rev. Evanston, Ill.: Northwestern University Press, 1964, 318 pp.

Jacobi, Jolande Szbekbacs, *Komplex, Archetypus, Symbol in der Psychologie C.G. Jung*. English: *Complex/Archetype/Symbol in the Psychology of C.G. Jung*. Trans. Ralph Manheim. Princeton, N.J.: Princeton University Press, 1971, 230 pp.

Jacobi, Jolande Szbekbacs, *Die Seelenmaske*. English: *Masks of the Soul*. Trans. Ean Beg. Grand Rapids, Michigan: Eerdmans, 1976, 94 pp.

Jacobi, Jolande Szbekbacs, *Der Weg zur Individuation*. English: *The Way of Individuation*. Trans. R.F.C. Hull. 1st ed. New York: Harcourt, Brace and World, 1967, 177 pp.

Kirsch, Hilde, ed., *The Well-Tended Tree: Essays into the Spirit of Our Time*. New York: Putnam for C.G. Jung Foundation for Analytical Psychology, 1971, 390 pp.

Kirsch, James, *The Reluctant Prophet*. Los Angeles: Sherbourne Press, 1973, 214 pp.

Sanford, John A., *The Invisible Partners: How the Male and Female in Each of Us Affects our Relationships*. New York: Paulist Press, 1980, 139 pp.

Scott-Maxwell, Florida (Pier), *Women and Sometimes Men*. New York: Harper and Row, 1971, 207 pp.

Stevens, Anthony, *Archetype: A Natural History of the Self*. London: Routledge & Kegan, 1982, 324 pp.

Wheelwright, Joseph B., ed., *The Reality of the Psyche*. New York: Putnam for the C.G. Jung Foundation for Analytical Psychology, 1968, 304 pp.

Zeller, Max, *The Dream: The Vision of the Night*. Ed. Janet Dallett. Los Angeles: Analytical Psychology Club of Los Angeles, 1975, 183 pp.

VIII Essays in Applied Psychology: General

Abell, Walter, *The Collective Dream in Art: A Psycho-Historical Theory of Culture Based on Relations between the Arts, Psychology, and the Social Sciences*. 1st Schocken ed. New York: Schocken Books, 1957, 378 pp.

Aronson, Alex, *Psyche and Symbol in Shakespeare*. Bloomington: Indiana University Press, 1972, 343 pp.

Baynes, Helton Godwin, *Analytical Psychology and the English Mind: and Other Papers*. Ed. Anne Baynes. London: Methuen, 1950, 242 pp.

Baynes, Helton Godwin, *Germany Possessed*. London: J. Cape. 1941. New York: AMS Press, 1972, 305 pp.

Bertine, Eleanor, *Human Relationships: in the Family, in Friendship, in Love*. 1st ed. New York: Longmans, Green, 1958, 237 pp.

Bickman, Martin, *The Unsounded Centre: Jungian Studies in American Romanticism*. Chapel Hill: University of North Carolina Press, 1980, 182 pp.

Bodkin, Maud, *Archetypal Patterns in Poetry: Psychological Studies of Imagination*. London: Oxford University Press, 1934, 340 pp.

Brivic, Sheldon, *Joyce between Freud and Jung*. Port Washington, N.Y.: Kennikat Press, 1980, 226 pp.

Castillejo, Irene Claremont de, *Knowing Woman: A Feminine Psychology*. New York: Harper and Row, 1973, 188 pp.

Edinger, Edward F., *Melville's Moby-Dick: A Jungian Commentary: An American Nekyia*. New York: New Directions Publishing Co., 1978, 150 pp.

Engelsman, Joan Chamberlain, *The Feminine Dimension of the Divine*. 1st ed. Philadelphia: Westminster Press, 1979, 203 pp.

Franz, Marie-Louise von, *Alchemical Active Imagination*. Irving, Texas: Spring Publications, 1979, 116 pp.

Franz, Marie-Louise von, ed., *Aurora Consurgens, A Document Attributed to Thomas Aquinas on the Problem of Opposites in Alchemy*. Trans. R.F.C. Hull and A.S.B. Glover. New York: Pantheon Books, 1966, 555 pp.

Franz, Marie-Louise von, *Individuation in Fairy Tales*. Zurich: Spring Publications, 1977, 189 pp.

Franz, Marie-Louise von, *An Introduction to the Interpretation of Fairy Tales.* New York: Spring Publications, 1970, n.p.

Franz, Marie-Louise von, *A Psychological Interpretation of the Golden Ass of Apuleius.* 2nd ed., completely rev. Irving, Texas: Spring Publications, University of Dallas, 1980, 218 pp.

Franz, Marie-Louise von, *Shadow and Evil in Fairy Tales.* New York: Spring Publications.The Analytical Psychology Club of New York, Inc., 1974, 284 pp.

Fritz, Donald W., ed., *Perspectives on Creativity and the Unconscious.* Oxford, Ohio: Miami University, 1980, 116 pp.

Gallant, Christine, *Blake and the Assimilation of Chaos.* Princeton, N.J.: Princeton University Press, 1978, 198 pp.

Gordon, Rosemary, *Dying and Creating: A Search for Meaning.* London: Society of Analytical Psychology, 1978, 186 pp.

Greene, Thayer A., *Modern Man in Search of Manhood.* New York: Association Press, 1967, 128 pp.

Grinnell, Robert, *Alchemy in a Modern Woman: A Study in the Contrasexual Archetype.* Zurich: Spring Publications, 1973, 181 pp.

Hall, Nor, *The Moon and the Virgin: Reflections on the Archetypal Feminine.* 1st ed. New York: Harper and Row, 1980, 284 pp.

Hamaker-Zondag, Karen, *Psyche en Astrologisch Symbool.* English: *Astro-psychology: Astrological Symbolism and the Human Psyche.* Trans. from the Dutch by Transcript. Wellingborough: Aquarian Press, 1980, 224 pp.

Hannah, Barbara, *Striving towards Wholeness.* New York: Putnam for the C.G. Jung Foundation for Analytical Psychology, 1971, 316 pp.

Harding, Mary Esther, *The Way of All Women: A Psychological Interpretation.* New York: Harper and Row, 1970, 314 pp.

Harding, Mary Esther, *Woman's Mysteries, Ancient and Modern: A Psychological Interpretation of the Feminine Principle as Portrayed in Myth, Story, and Dreams.* New York: Harper and Row, 1971, 256 pp.

Hillman, James, *Healing Fiction.* Barrytown, N.Y.: Station Hill Press, 1983, n.p.

Jacobson, Helmuth, ed., *Archetypische Motive in der chassidischen mystik. English: Timeless Documents of the Soul.* Evanston, Ill.: Northwestern University Press, 1968, 263 pp.

Jaffe, Aniela, *Apparitions: An Archetypal Approach to Death Dreams and Ghosts.* Irving, Texas: Spring Publications, 1979, 214 pp.

Johnson, Robert, *He: Understanding Masculine Psychology, Based on the Legend of Parsifal and His Search for the Grail, and Using Jungian Psychological Concepts.* New York: Harper and Row, 1974, 83 pp.

Johnson, Robert, *She: Understanding Feminine Psychology, An Inter-pretation Based on the Myth of Amor and Psyche and Using Jungian Psychological Concepts*. New York: Harper and Row, 1976, 72 pp.

Jung, C.G. and K. Kerenyi, *Einfuhrung in das Wesen der Mythologie*. English: *Essays on a Science of Mythology: the Myth of the Divine Child and the Mysteries of Eleusis*. Trans. R.F.C. Hull. Rev. ed. Princeton, N.J.: Princeton University Press, 1963, 200 pp.

Jung, Emma, *Animus and Anima*. Dallas: Spring Publications, 1981, 94 pp.

Jung, Emma and Marie-Louise von Franz, *Die Graalslegende in Psychologischer Sicht*. English: *The Grail Legend*. Trans. Andrea Dykes. New York: Putnam for the C.G. Jung Foundation for Analytical Psychology, 1970, 452 pp.

Kerenyi, Karl, *Der Ghottliche Arzt*. English: *Asklepios: Archetypal Image of the Physician's Existence*. Trans. Ralph Manheim. Princeton, N.J.: Princeton University Press, 1981, 151 pp.

Kerenyi, Karl, *Dionysos: Archetypal Image of Indestructible Life*. Trans. Ralph Manheim. Princeton, N.J.: Princeton University Press, 1976, 474 pp.

Kerenyi, Karl, *Eleusis: Archetypal Image of Mother and Daughter*. Trans. Ralph Manheim. New York: Schocken Books, 1967, 257 pp.

Kerenyi, Karl, *The Gods of the Greeks*. Trans. Norman Cameron. New York: Thames and Hudson, 1979, 304 pp.

Kerenyi, Karl, *Hermes der Seelenfuhrer*. English: *Hermes Guide of Souls: The Mythologem of the Masculine Source of Life*. Trans. Murray Stein. Zurich: Spring Publications, 1976, 104 pp.

Kerenyi, Karl, *Prometheus: Archetypal Image of Human Existence*. Trans. Ralph Manheim. New York: Bollingen Foundation, Pantheon Books, 1963, 152 pp.

Kerenyi, Karl et al., *Evil*, ed., Curatorium of the C.G. Jung Institute, Zurich. Trans. Ralph Manheim and Hildegard Nagel. Evanston, Ill.: Northwestern University Press, 1967, 265 pp.

Kirsch, James, *Shakespeare's Royal Self*. New York: Putnam for the C.G. Jung Foundation for Analytical Psychology, 1966, 422 pp.

Kotschnig, Elined Prys, *Womenhood in Myth and Life*. Washington: Inward Light, 1976, 32 pp.

Layard, John Willoughby, *A Celtic Quest: Sexuality and Soul in Individuation, a Depth-Psychology Study of the Mabinogion Legend of Culhwch and Olwen*. Rev. and ed. Anne S. Bosch. Zurich: Spring Publications, 1975, 254 pp.

Layard, John Willoughby, *The Lady of the Hare: Being a Study in the Healing Power of Dreams*. New York: AMS Press, 1977, 277 pp.

Layard, John Willoughby, *The Virgin Archetype*. New York: Spring Publications, 1972, 344 pp.

Lopez-Pedraza, Rafael, *Hermes and His Children*. Zurich: Spring Publications, 1977, 135 pp.

Luke, Helen M., *Dark Wood to White Rose: A Study of Meanings in Dante's Divine Comedy*. Pecos, N.M.: Dove Publications, 1975, 162 pp.

Luke, Helen M., *Through Defeat to Joy: The Novels of Charles Williams in the Light of Jungian Thought*. Three Rivers, Michigan: Apple Farm, 1980, 84 pp.

Luke, Helen M., *The Way of Woman, Ancient and Modern*. Three Rivers, Michigan: H.M. Luke, n.d., 60 pp.

Martin, Percival William, *Experiment in Depth: A Study of the Work of Jung, Eliot, and Toynbee*. Boston: Routledge & Kegan Paul, 1955, 275 pp.

Miller, David LeRoy, *The New Polytheism: Rebirth of the Gods and Goddesses*. 1st ed. New York: Harper and Row, 1974, 86 pp.

Monk, Patricia, *The Smaller Infinity: The Jungian Self in the Novels of Robertson Davies*. Toronto, Buffalo: University of Toronto Press, 1982, 214 pp.

Neumann, Erich, *Amor and Psyche: The Psychic Development of the Feminine: A Commentary on the Tale by Apuleius*. Trans. Ralph Manheim. Princeton, N.J.: Princeton University Press, 1956, 181 pp.

Neumann, Erich, *The Archetypal World of Henry Moore*. Trans. R.F.C. Hull. New York: Pantheon Books, 1959, 138 pp.

Neumann, Erich, *Umkreisung der Mitte*. English: *Art and the Creative Unconscious*. Trans. Ralph Manheim. Princeton, N.J.: Princeton University Press, 1959, 232 pp.

Neumann, Erich, *Kind: Struktur und Dynamik der werdenden Persönlichkeit*. English: *The Child: Structure and Dynamics of the Nascent Personality*. Trans. Ralph Manheim. New York: Putnam for C.G. Jung Foundation for Analytical Psychology, 1973, 221 pp.

Neumann, Erich, *Creative Man*. Trans. Eugene Rolfe. Princeton, N.J.: Princeton University Press, 1979, 264 pp.

Neumann, Erich, *Tiefenpsychologie und neue Ethik*. English: *Depth Psychology and a New Ethic*. Trans. Eugene Rolfe. New York: Harper and Row, 1969, 158 pp.

Neumann, Erich, *Die Grosse Mutter*. English: *The Great Mother: An Analysis of the Archetype*. Trans. Ralph Manheim. Princeton,

N.J.: Princeton University Press, 1974, 379 pp.

Neumann, Erich, *The Origins and History of Consciousness*. Trans. R.F.C. Hull. New York: Pantheon Books, 1973, 493 pp.

Nichols, Sallie, *Jung and Tarot: An Archetypal Journey*. New York: S. Weiser, 1980, 393 pp.

Odajnyk, Walter, *Jung and Politics: The Political and Social Ideas of C.G. Jung*. New York: New York University Press, 1976, 190 pp.

Olney, James, *Metaphors of Self: The Meaning of Autobiography*. Princeton, N.J.: Princeton University Press, 1981, 342 pp.

Olney, James, *The Rhizome and the Flower: The Perennial Philosophy, Yeats and Jung*. Berkeley: University of California Press, 1980, 379 pp.

O'Neill, Timothy R., *The Individuated Hobbit: Jung, Tolkien, and the Archetypes of Middle-Earth*. Boston: Houghton Mifflin, 1979, 200 pp.

Pauli, W., *The Influence of Archetypal Ideas on the Scientific Theories of Kepler*. In: Bollingen Series, v.51. New York: Pantheon, 1955, 247 pp.

Pelgrin, Mark, *And A Time to Die*. Ed. Sheila Moon and Elizabeth B. Howes. London: Routledge and Paul, 1961, 159 pp.

Perry, John Weir, *The Far Side of Madness*. Englewood Cliffs, N.J.: Prentice-Hall, 1974, 177 pp.

Perry, John Weir, *Lord of the Four Quarters: Myths of the Royal Father*. New York: G. Braziller, 1966, 272 pp.

Perry, John Weir, *Roots of Renewal in Myth and Madness*. 1st ed. San Francisco: Jossey-Bass Publishers, 1976, 256 pp.

Perry, John Weir, *The Self in Psychotic Process: Its Symbolization in Schizophrenia*. Berkeley: University of California Press, 1953, 184 pp.

Philipson, Morris H., *Outline of a Jungian Aesthetics*. Evanston, Ill.: Northwestern University Press, 1963, 214 pp.

Philp, Howard Littleton, *Jung and the Problem of Evil*. New York: R.M. McBride Co., 1958, 271 pp.

Progoff, Ira, *The Death and Rebirth of Psychology: An Integrative Evaluation of Freud, Adler, Jung and Rank and the Impact of their Culminating Insights on Modern Man*. New York: McGraw-Hill, 1973, 275 pp.

Progoff, Ira, *Jung, Synchronicity, and Human Destiny: Noncausal Dimensions of Human Experience*. New York: Julian Press, 1973, 176 pp.

Roscher, Wilhelm Heinrich, *Ephialtes*. English: *Pan and the Nightmare*. Trans. A.V. O'Brien. New York: Spring Publications, 1972, 88 pp.

Serrano, Miguel, *El Circulo Hermbetico*. English: *C.G. Jung and Hermann Hesse: A Record of Two Friendships*. Trans. Frank MacShane. New York: Schocken Books, 1966, 112 pp.

Singer, June K., *Androgyny: Toward a New Theory of Sexuality*. Garden City, N.Y.: Anchor Press/Doubleday, 1976, 371 pp.

Spiegelman, Marvin, *The Tree: Tales in Psycho-Mythology*, 1st ed. Los Angeles: Phoenix House, 1974, 464 pp.

Steuernagel, Gertrude A., *Political Philosophy as Therapy: Marcuse Reconsidered*. Westport, Conn.: Greenwood Press, 1979, 147 pp.

Stroud, Jean and Gail Thomas, eds., *Images of the Untouched: Virginity in Psyche, Myth, and Community*. Dallas, Texas: Spring Publications, 1982, 201 pp.

Trinick, John, *The Fire-Tried Stone (Signum Atque Signatum): An Enquiry into the Development of a Symbol*. Marazion, Wordens of Cornwall, London: Stuart and Watkins, 1967, 138 pp.

Turner, Dixie M., *A Jungian Psychoanalytic Interpretation of William Faulkner's As I Lay Dying*. Washington: University Press of America, 1981, 99 pp.

Van der Post, Laurens, *A Mantis Carol*. New York: Morrow, 1975, 165 pp.

Weaver, Rix, *The Old Wise Woman: A Study of Active Imagination*. New York: Putnam for the C.G. Jung Foundation for Analytical Psychology, 1973, 176 pp.

Wheelwright, Jane, *The Death of a Woman*. New York: St. Martin's Press, 1981, n.p.

Wickes, Frances Gillespy, *The Inner World of Childhood: A Study in Analytical Psychology*. New York: Mentor Books, 1966, 304 pp.

Wickes, Frances Gillespy, *The Inner World of Choice*. Englewood Cliffs, N.J.: Prentice-Hall, Inc., 1963, 318 pp.

Wickes, Frances Gillespy, *The Inner World of Man*. New York: Farrar and Rinehart, Inc., 1938, 313 pp.

Wilhelm, Richard, trans., *The Secret of the Golden Flower: A Chinese Book of Life*. New York: Harcourt, Brace and World, 1962, 149 pp.

Willeford, William, *The Fool and His Scepter: A Study in Clowns and Jesters and their Audience*. Evanston, Ill.: Northwestern University Press, 1969, 265 pp.

IX Essays in Applied Psychology: Religion

Bertine, Eleanor, M. Esther Harding, and Edward C. Whitmont, *Jung's Approach to Religion: Three Papers*. New York: Analytical Psychology Club, 1959, 49 leaves.

Campbell, Joseph, *The Hero with a Thousand Faces.* 2nd ed. Princeton, N.J.: Princeton University Press, 1972, 416 pp.

Champernowne, Irene, *The One and Only Me.* Niles, Ill.: Argus Communications, 1975, 62 pp.

Cox, David, *Jung and St. Paul: A Study of the Doctrine of Justification By Faith and Its Relation to the Concept of Individuation.* New York: Association Press, 1959, 357 pp.

Cox, David, *Modern Psychology: The Teachings of Carl Gustav Jung.* New York: Barnes and Noble, 1968, 181 pp.

Daking, D.C., *Jungian Psychology and Modern Spiritual Thought.* Anglo-Eastern Publishing Co.,n.d. 133 pp.

Davidson, Ronald H. and Richard Day, *Symbol and Realization: A Contribution to the Study of Magic and Healing.* Berkeley: Center for South and Southeast Asia Studies, University of California, 1974, 135 pp.

Franz, Marie-Louise von, *Passio sanctarum Perpetuae et Felicitatis.* English: *The Passion of Perpetua.* Irving, Texas: Spring Publications, 1980, 81 pp.

Franz, Marie-Louise von, *Patterns of Creativity Mirrored in Creation Myths.* New York: Spring Publications, 1972, 250 pp.

Franz, Marie Louise von, *The Problem of the Puer Aeternus.* New York: Spring Publications, 1970, n.p.

Franz, Marie Louise von, *Problems of the Feminine in Fairytales.* New York: Spring Publications (The Analytical Psychology Club of New York, Inc.), 1972, 194 pp.

Franz, Marie-Louise von, *The Psychological Meaning of Redemption Motifs in Fairytales.* Toronto: Inner City Books, 1980, 124 pp.

Goldbrunner, Josef, *Cure of Mind and Cure of Soul.* New York: Pantheon, 1958, 127 pp.

Goldbrunner, Josef, *Holiness is Wholeness and Other Essays.* Notre Dame, Indiana: University of Notre Dame Press, 1964, 101 pp.

Goldbrunner, Josef, *Individuation: A Study of the Depth Psychology of Carl Gustav Jung.* Trans. Stanley Godman. Notre Dame, Ind.: University of Notre Dame Press, 1964, 204 pp.

Goldbrunner, Josef, *Realization: Anthropology of Pastoral Care.* Trans. Paul C. Bailey and Elisabeth Reinecke. Notre Dame, Ind.: University of Notre Dame Press, 1966, 221 pp.

Hanna, Charles Bartruff, *The Face of the Deep: The Religious Ideas of C.G. Jung.* Philadelphia: Westminster Press, 1967, 203 pp.

Harding, Mary Esther, *Journey into Self.* New York: Longmans, Green and Co., 1956, 301 pp.

Heisig, James W., *Imago Dei: A Study of C.G. Jung's Psychology of Religion*. Lewisburg, Pa.: Bucknell University Press, 1979, 253 pp.

Henderson, Joseph L., *Thresholds of Initiation*. 1st paperback ed. Middletown, Conn.: Wesleyan University Press, 1979, 260 pp.

Henderson, Joseph L. and Maud Oakes, *The Wisdom of the Serpent: The Myths of Death, Rebirth and Resurrection*. New York: G. Braziller, 1963, 262 pp.

Herzog, Edgar, *Psyche and Death: Archaic Myths and Modern Dreams in Analytical Psychology*. Trans. David Cox and Eugene Rolfe. 1st American ed. New York: Putnam for the C.G. Jung Foundation for Analytical Psychology, 1966, 224 pp.

Hillman, James, ed., *Facing the Gods*. Irving, Texas: Spring Publications, 1980, 172 pp.

Hillman, James, *Insearch: Psychology and Religion*. Irving, Texas: Spring Publications, 1967, 126 pp.

Hillman, James et al., *Puer Papers*. Irving, Texas: Spring Publications, 1979, 246 pp.

Hillman, James, *Re-visioning Psychology*. New York: J. Wiley, 1975, 266 pp.

Hostie, Raymond, *Religion and the Psychology of Jung*. Trans. G.R. Lamb. New York: Sheed and Ward, 1957, 249 pp.

Howes, Elizabeth Boyden, *Intersection and Beyond: Twelve Lectures on the Commingling of Religious Values and the Insights of Analytical Psychology*. Rev. ed. San Francisco, Ca.: Guild for Psychological Studies, 1971, 198 pp.

Howes, Elizabeth Boyden and Sheila Moon, *Man the Choicemaker*. Philadelphia: Westminster Press, 1973, 218 pp.

Kelsey, Morton T., *Christo-psychology*. New York: Crossroad, 1982, 154 pp.

Kelsey, Morton T., *Companions on the Inner Way: A Guide to Spiritual Direction*. New York: Crossroad, 1982.

Kelsey, Morton T., *Prophetic Ministry: The Psychology and Spirituality of Pastoral Care*. New York: Crossroad, 1982, 210 pp.

Kluger, Rivkah Scharf, *Psyche and Bible: Three Old Testament Themes*. Zurich: Spring Publications, 1974, 144 pp.

Kluger, Rivkah Scharf, *Satan in the Old Testament*. Trans. Hildegard Nagel. Evanston, Ill.: Northwestern University Press, 1967, 173 pp.

Luke, Helen M., *The Inner Story: Myth and Symbol in the Bible and Literature*. New York: Crossroad, 1982, 118 pp.

Meier, Carl Alfred, *Jung's Analytical Psychology and Religion*. Carbondale, Ill.: Southern Illinois University Press, 1977, 80 pp.

Moon, Sheila, *A Magic Dwells: A Poetic and Psychological Study of the Navaho Emergence Myth.* 1st ed. Middletown, Ca.: Wesleyan University Press, 1970, 206 pp.

Moon, Sheila, *Out of the Darkness: Navaho Myth and Psychological Growth.* Middletown, Conn.: Guild for Psychological Studies, 1963, 31 pp.

Mooney, Lucindi Frances, *Storming Eastern Temples: A Psychological Exploration of Yoga.* 1st ed. Wheaton, Ill.: Theosophical Publishing House, 1976, 212 pp.

Moreno, Antonio, *Jung, Gods, and Modern Man.* Notre Dame, Ind.: University of Notre Dame Press, 1970, 274 pp.

Radin, Paul, *The Trickster: A Study in American Indian Mythology.* New York: Schocken Books, 1972, 211 pp.

Sandner, Donald, *Navaho Symbols of Healing.* 1st Harvest/HBJ ed. New York: Harcourt Brace Jovanovich, 1979, 290 pp.

Sanford, John A., *The Man Who Wrestled with God: Light from the Old Testament on the Psychology of Individuation.* New York: Paulist Press, 1981, 119 pp.

Schaer, Hans, *Religion and the Cure of Souls in Jung's Psychology.* Trans. R.F.C. Hull. New York: Pantheon Books, 1950, 221 pp.

Singer, June K., *The Unholy Bible: A Psychological Interpretation of William Blake.* New York: Harper and Row, 1970, 270 pp.

Ulanov, Ann Belford, *The Feminine in Jungian Psychology and in Christian Theology.* Evanston, Ill.: Northwestern University Press, 1971, 347 pp.

Ulanov, Ann Belford, *Religion and the Unconscious.* Philadelphia: Westminster Press, 1975, 287 pp.

Von der Heydt, Vera, *Prospects for the Soul: Soundings in Jungian Psychology and Religion.* London: Darton, Longman and Todd, 1976, 110 pp.

Weatherhead, Leslie Dixon, *Psychology, Religion, and Healing.* Rev. ed. New York: Abingdon Press, 1952, 543 pp.

White, Victor, *God and the Unconscious.* Cleveland: World Publishing Co., 1952, 287 pp.

White, Victor, *Soul and Psyche: An Enquiry into the Relationship of Psychotherapy and Religion.* New York: Harper, 1960, 312 pp.

Whitmont, Edward C., *The Symbolic Quest: Basic Concepts of Analytical Psychology.* Princeton, N.J.: Princeton University Press, 1969, 336 pp.

Wiggins, James B., ed., *Religion as Story.* 1st ed. New York: Harper and Row, 1975, 203 pp.

Wiggins, James B., ed., *Religion as Story*. 1st ed. New York: Harper and
     Row, 1975, 203 pp.

INDEX

Academic psychologist (Jung as), xii, 17–18
Acquired characteristics, 48–49
Active imagination, 60–61
Adaptation, 50–51
Adler, Alfred, 58
Aesthetics, 3–4, 64
Affects (see also Feeling), 6–7, 15–16, 74–75, 85, 105
Aggressive instincts, 71
Aim-inhibition, 65–66
Alchemy, 31, 88, 94, 98, 115
Ambivalence, 47, 104
Amplification, 84
Anal, character, 34
Analyst, attitude of, 18–19, 52–53, 56–57
'Analytical Psychology', xii–xiii, 58–59, 99–100, 118–19
Anima(-us, -i), 37–39, 80, 83–84, 102, 117
Animal Gods, 34, 83
Animism, 43
Anti-Freudian (Jung as), 9, 45–55, 62–63, 72–73, 93
Anti-semitism, 68–69
Anthropology, 76–77, 97
Anthropomorphization, 39
Anxiety, 19, 50–51, 63, 114–115
A-phenomenon, 9
Archetypes
        and instincts, 32–33, 61–62, 64–65, 67, 75–76
        and religion, 10, 29–30, 78–80, 82–111
        and symbols, 27–28, 31, 35–36, 58–59, 118–120
Art, 10–11, 63–64
Aryan unconscious (see Nietzsche)
Association experiments (association method), 9–11
Associations, classification of, 11
Astrology, 99–100, 106
Attention, 9, 16
Attitudinal types, 62, 82
Automatism, 76–77

Autonomous complex, 64, 81, 85, 119

Balance, 65, 85
Biology, 49, 58, 61, 67, 98, 102
Birth, 38
Blood, 95–96
Body, 85
Buddhism (see Eastern Religion)

Castration, 50
Catholicism, 33, 84, 94–97, 101
Childbirth, 21, 39
Children, 47–48, 54
Christ, 103–104
Christianity, 43, 64, 69, 87, 108–111
Civilization, 61, 79
Clang (see Sound association)
Collective unconscious, 55, 66–67, 75
Compensation, 62–63, 70, 83, 85, 117
Complex, 6–7, 12–13, 29, 64
Complex constellation, 14, 21, 82
Consciousness, 39, 63, 82, 97, 104
Consensus gentium, 82, 93, 111
Constellation, 13–14, 72–74, 108
Contradictions, 64–65
Contra-sexual, the, 16, 37
Creative activity, 10–11, 52
Crime, 18

Dancing, 32
'Dark' side, the (see Shadow)
Death, 40–41, 119–20
Depression, 42–43, 115
Destructive instincts (see Aggressive instincts)
Determinism (see Reductionism)
Developmental factors, 48, 110
Devil, 36, 46, 104
Dissociation, 51
Dogma, 34, 44, 83, 86
Dreams, 14–15, 53, 63, 72–75
Dream, great, 83–84, 86, 89, 110, 116, 118

Eastern Religion, 108–109
Eating, symbolism of, 72–73
Eclecticism, 71
Education, 92

Ego (see also Self), 64, 82, 85, 97, 102, 119–120
Egocentric reactions, 17
Ego-complex, 111
Emotions (see Affects and Feelings)
Enantiodromia, 109
Endopsychic factors, 99
Energy, 47–48, 79
Equilibrium, 85, 102
Erotic complex, 33
Eucharist (see also Mass), 40
Evil, 83, 85, 104, 108–109, 120
Evolution of mind, 54–55, 69
Extraversion, 77

Family constellation, 54
Fantasy, 19, 27–28, 63, 69, 78
Father, 114–116
Faust, 77, 116
Feeling (see also Affects), 95
Feminine deity, 88–90, 94–95, 108, 111
Fetishism, 95, 114, 118
First World War, 85
Fish, 105–106
Folklore (see Myths)
Fourfoldness, 42, 93
Free association, 63
Freud, Sigmund, 25, 35, 47, 86, 101, 117–118

Genetic source, 85
Genital sexuality (see Sexuality)
Germany, 28, 30, 59, 69–71
Gnostics, 7, 97
God, image, 26, 30, 75, 87, 110
Goethe, 120
Greek religion, 43, 64, 89, 103

Hallucination(s), 5–7
Hermetic philosophy (see Alchemy)
Hero, 31, 33, 36, 97, 103, 118
Heterosexuality, 47
Hitler, 69–70
Holy ghost, 35, 89, 109–110
Homosexuality, 38, 47–48
Hypnosis, 10, 56
Hysteria, 8–9, 18, 46–47, 68

Idea of God (see God)
Identification, 62, 74
Incest, 23, 34–35, 50, 118
Indians, 72
Individual development, 32, 64, 77
Individuation, 58, 62, 86, 91, 96, 105, 108, 113
Infantile sexuality (see Polymorphism)
Inferior function, 76–77, 113
Inherited ideas (see Archetypes)
Insanity (see Psychoses)
Instinct, 65–68
Instincts, sexual, 48
Interpretation, 78
Introjection, 95–96
Introversion, 77
Intuition, 64, 66

Jesus, 22, 36, 39, 91, 94
Jewish psychology, 68–70
Jews, 69–71, 108, 118

Kant, I., 59, 70

Libido, 33–34, 48, 69
Literature, 18
Lucifer, 120

Magic, 32, 94–95
Magna Mater, 86, 90
Mandala, 87, 105, 116, 119
Marriage, 102
Masculine attributes, 107–108
Mass, the Catholic, 91–92, 94–98
Matrix, unconscious, 79–80
Meaning, 99
Mediation, 98
Melancholia, 114
Memory, 51, 60, 114
Metaphor, 92
Metapsychology, 58, 63, 79
Middle Ages, 56
Mithraism, 70, 101
Morality, 49, 51, 56, 59–61, 72, 79
Mother, symbols of, 35–36, 37–42, 79, 114
Mystery, 94
Mystical ideas, 5–6, 61–62, 76

Myth, personal, 26, 121
Myths, 28, 67–68

Nature, 111, 120
Nazism, 68
Neurosis, 43, 49, 62, 76
Nietzsche, 7, 31, 37–38, 40, 103, 116
Numbers, 78, 85
Numinosity, 82, 84, 115, 117

Object relations, 114
Objectivity, 64, 74, 78
Occult, xii, 1–7, 82, 115
Oedipus, 27–28, 47–48, 50, 74
Opposites, 64–65, 99–100
Orientation, unconscious, 64
Original sin, 83

Paranoia, 117
Parents, 49
Perceptual consciousness, 67
Persona, 77, 80, 115
Personal unconscious, 69
Personality, 10, 100, 119
Phallus, 31–32, 63
Phenomenology, 48, 50, 100–101, 107, 120
Philosopher, 75, 88, 104
Phylogenesis, 83
Phobias, 66
Plato, 89–90, 92
Poetry, 38, 103
Polymorphism, sexual, 47–49, 63
Possession by demons, 46
Post-reformation period, 110–111
Pre-Oedipal fantasy, 35
Pregnancy, 35
Primary instincts (see Instincts)
Primary processes, 27–28, 58–59
Primitive humans, 41, 52, 67, 70, 73
Primordial images, 73, 76, 80
Prognostication, 72
Projection, 39, 70–71, 74
Prospective functions, 52, 73
Protestantism, 33, 92–93, 96
Psychic reality (see also Reality), 95–96

Psyche, 27, 31, 60, 79, 105
Psychoanalysis (see Freud)
Psychological truth, 28
Psychoses, 26, 85, 111
Psychopathology, 13, 116
Psychophysical experiments (see WAT)
Psychotherapy, 16, 54, 57–58, 62, 65, 78, 117
Puberty, 116

Quaternity, 42, 85–86, 89–90, 93, 102

Racial inheritance (see also Collective unconscious), 83
Rationality, 35, 61–62, 69, 84, 95
Reality, 79–80
Reaction, 17
Rebirth, 35–36, 42
Redemption, 106
Reductionism, 26, 66–67
Regression, 32, 39, 42, 52
Religion as cure, 50, 59, 67, 76
Repression, 5, 18–19
Resistances, 52, 120

Sacrifice, 42–44, 95–96
Schizophrenia, 2–3, 21, 32, 53, 87
School complex, 54, 115
Science, 61, 65, 103–4
Secondary processes, 12, 27, 58
Self (see also Individuation), 36–37, 39, 97, 101
Semiotic, 58–59, 62, 78, 96
Sexual complexes, 18–19, 58
Sexual instincts, 47–48, 58–59
Sexuality, 29–30, 71
Sexual differences, 16–17
Shadow, 22, 34, 85, 89, 101
Sleep, 10, 14
Slips of the tongue, 63
Society, 75
Sociobiology, 67
Socrates, 54–55
Sound associations (sound reactions), 12–13
Split personality, 4–7, 10, 19, 115
Stimulus words, 10–11
Subconscious mind (see unconscious)
Subjective type, 17

Subliminal, the, 8, 29
Suggestion, 63
Sun-god, 31, 40, 85
Symbolism, 58–59, 73–74, 83–84, 109
Symptom-formation, 23
Synchronicity, 99–100, 110, 116, 120

Teleological function, 7, 38, 58–59, 61–63, 72
Theology, 78, 88, 103, 120
Transcendent function, 60–65
Transference, 52, 62–63
Transformation, 30–31, 35, 94–95
Traumatic experiences, 46, 51
Trinity, 85–86, 89–90
Type psychology, 79, 100

Unconscious, the (see also Collective unconscious), 20, 64
Unicellular organisms, 49
Union of opposites, 38, 64, 106

Value judgments, 58
Value, psychic, 103
Virgin, the, 31

Visions, 85–87, 117, 119

Wagner, R., 40–41
War, 75
WAT, 9–11, 50, 82
Will, 20–21, 32, 107
Wisdom, 108
Wish fulfilment, 63–64, 74–75

Zosimos, 95–98